A NARRATIVE OF POLITICAL PARTIES IN BELIZE

A NARRATIVE OF POLITICAL PARTIES IN BELIZE

Lawrence Vernon

Belize City

2017

Self-Publish 2017

ISBN: 978-976-95563-7-9

Book Cover, Typography, Design and Layout of book by Reynolds Desktop Publishing

Email: reynoldsdesktoppublishing@gmail.com

Photos courtesy of Belize Billboard and Dylan Vernon

This book was published with financial support by the Belize National Institute of Culture and History (NICH)

CONTENTS

Abbreviations..8

Preface... 10

Foreword 13

Acknowledgements... 16

Prologue 18

Section One – Emergence of the People's United Party 24

From the People's Committee to Independence 24

The People's United Party 32

Section Two – Emergence of Opposition Parties.................... 129

The National Party – 1951... 129

The Honduran Independence Party – 1956.................... 138

The National Independence Party – 1958............................ 143

The Democratic Agricultural and Labour Party – 1958 (Later called The Christian Democratic Party) 175

The Peoples' Independent Party – 1968............................... 180

The United Black Association for Development – 1968..... 180

The People's Development Movement – 1969.................... 187

Section Three – The Rise of the United Democratic Party..... 190

The United Democratic Party – 1973 190

Section Four – Small Parties Since 1974................................ 203

The Corozal United Front – 1974... 203

The Corozal United Party – 1978.. 203

The Toledo Progressive Party – 1979................................... 203

The Christian Democratic Party – 1982 203

The Belize Popular Party – 1988...................................204

The San Pedro United Movement – 1989.............................204

Section Five – Third Party Hopefuls..............................205

The National Alliance for Belizean Rights – 1991...............205

The People's Democratic Party – 1995.............................210

The National Reality Truth Creation Party – 1998..............211

We the People Reform Movement – 2003.............................211

Vision Inspired By the People – 2005.............................212

The People's National Party – 2007..............................214

The National Reform Party – 2007................................214

National Belize Alliance – 2007.................................216

The Party of Christians Pursuing Reform – 2007.................217

Belize Unity Alliance – 2011.....................................217

Belize Progressive Party – 2015.................................217

Section Six – 2015 – A Year for Elections.......................218

Conclusion...220

Appendices...221

Appendix I..221

The Institution of Adult Suffrage...............................221

Appendix II...223

The Webster Proposals...223

Appendix III..225

Results of General Elections 1984 – 2015........................225

Index of Political Parties......................................228

References...229

Further Reading...230

End Notes..231

About The Author 235

Figure 1 - Antonio Soberanis.. 23
Figure 2 - John Smith 34
Figure 3 - Philip Goldson   Figure 4 - Leigh Richardson 36
Figure 5 - Richardson & Goldson released from prison. 46
Figure 6 - Nicholas Pollard.. 63
Figure 7 - George Price.. 66
Figure 8 - Albert Cattouse 71
Figure 9 - George Price.. 79
Figure 10 - Carl Rogers... 84
Figure 11 - Gwendolyn Lizarraga... 87
Figure 12 - Belize gaining self-government, 1964 100
Figure 13 - Said Musa.. 119
Figure 14 - Herman Jex... 141
Figure 15 - Herbert Fuller.. 143
Figure 16 - Philip Goldson... 152
Figure 17 - Evan X Hyde.. 181
Figure 18 - Dean Lindo 191
Figure 19 - Manuel Esquivel... 196
Figure 20 - Dean Barrow 219

Abbreviations

BPP   Belize Popular Party // Belize Progressive Party

BUA   Belize Unity Alliance

CDU   Christian Democratic Union

CDP   Christian Democratic Party

CUF   Corozal United Front

CUP   Corozal United Party

DALP   Democratic Agricultural and Labour Party

GWU   General Workers Union

HIP   Honduran Independence Party

NABR   National Alliance for Belizean Rights

NBA   National Belize Alliance

NIP   National Independence Party

NP   National Party

NRP   National Reform Party

PAC   People's Action Committee

PC   People's Committee

PDM   People's Development Movement

PDP	People's Democratic Party
PIP	People's Independent Party
PNP	People's National Party
PUP	People's United Party
RAM	Revolitical Action Movement
SPUM	San Pedro United Movement
TPP	Toledo Progressive Party
UBAD	United Black Association for Development
UDP	United Democratic Party
VIP	Vision Inspired by the People
WTP	We the People Reform Movement

PREFACE

The main event which was responsible for the political awakening in Belize, and which in fact was responsible for sparking the whole nationalist movement in Belize, was the devaluation of the country's currency on December 31, 1949. It has to be realized, however, that in as much as organized political parties in Belize were non-existent prior to 1950 Antonio Soberanis[i] succeeded in the 1930s to form a revolutionary movement.

Underlying and preceding devaluation were also other relevant factors:

- The first organized workers union in Belize, the General Workers Union, was receiving its first successes and recognition as a valuable organization during the years 1947 to 1949.
- The *Belize Billboard*, one of the country's two newspapers, was vigorously airing the cause of labor and the masses.
- Since 1945 the Legislative Council had been objecting to the level of financial dependence, in the form of grants-in-aid, which Belize was receiving from the United Kingdom.
- Steps towards self-determination could be seen from the committee which was working from 1947 on constitutional proposals for adult suffrage, an elected majority in the legislature, and an elected executive.

The devaluation of the dollar by Governor Sir Ronald Garvey was facetiously termed a "New Year's gift" by the *Belize*

10

Billboard, and the event triggered a political transformation which might not have otherwise taken place so early. What started as a mere protest against devaluation escalated into a general assault against the entire colonial system, especially when some of the reasons for devaluation were revealed in the Financial Secretary's report of 1949:

- American demand for mahogany and chicle slumped in 1949 resulting in the trading trend shifting from the dollar area to the sterling area.
- The producers of pine lumber, grapefruit and fruit juices became aware that their export market in the sterling area was adversely affected by the devaluation of sterling, while the dollar was not devalued.
- There was a lack of confidence in the dollar, which was evident in many different ways.

It is significant to note that the majority of the members of the Legislative Council had voted against devaluation, but the Governor exercised his reserve powers and passed the resolution. This had the immediate reaction of being branded as dictatorial precipitating some 1,500 citizens to defy heavy rains to attend a meeting at the Battlefield[1] on the night of December 31, 1949. A resolution was hastily passed demanding that the Belize dollar be restored to parity with the U. S. A. dollar. More importantly, at that very time a People's Committee was formed to take up the "Dollar Back" fight.

---

[1]The site of today's Battlefield Park in Belize City.

Subsequent years were to see various constitutional advances like the introduction of universal adult suffrage; the title of the legislature restored to that of Legislative Assembly; an increase in the number of electoral seats; the Membership and Ministerial systems, self-government; and eventual independence.

This chronological narrative, which is intended to be exclusively of political parties which were formed in Belize since 1950 (of which there were 26), is comprised mostly of edited, summarized and adapted versions of the opinions expressed by the major players from direct newspaper reports. Apart from the instances the author quotes authoritative historians, the views expressed are meant to be unbiased and do not in any way attempt to compare or contrast any one political party or faction or personality with another.

The events depicting the birth, growth and in some instances the demise of Belize's political parties described in this book, with the exception of the two mass parties the People's United Party and the United Democratic Party which conclude at Independence in 1981, are extant up to the year of publication. The author has every intention of continuing to narrate on those two mass parties in a timely manner.

Although the country was formerly known as British Honduras until the name was officially changed to Belize in 1973, for purposes of consistency and clarity the name Belize is used throughout this work, except in instances of direct quotes from other sources.

FOREWORD

Belize's parliamentary democracy is best exemplified by its two-party system, with the two leading political parties the People's United Party, 1950 and the National Independence Party, 1958 and its successor the United Democratic Party, 1973, alternating their predominance in government and as the loyal opposition. It may come as a surprise to many that since the 1950s some 26 parties, many of them long-defunct and now forgotten, have sought to influence the political future of the country. In this work, Lawrence Vernon, a distinguished librarian and political historian, sets out to chronicle the development of these parties in an effort to ensure that their leaders, manifestos, and impact are not left locked away in archives or in the memories of a few.

After introductions which rightly so identify the 1949 devaluation of the British Honduras Dollar as the match that lit the nationalist fires and underscores the importance of Antonio Soberanis Gomez as the father of both trade unionism and nationalism, the First and Third Sections are devoted to the rise of the People's United Party (P.U.P.) and the United Democratic Party (U.D.P.) from their founding (1950 for the former and 1973 for the latter) up to independence. Section Two describes the rise of those parties that were in opposition to the P.U.P. starting with the National Party in 1951 and ending with the People's Development Movement in 1969. Section Four briefly tells the stories of six small parties that were active between 1974 and 1981. Section Five examines 10 parties that have sought to become viable third parties, beginning with the National Alliance for Belizean Rights in 1991. The book ends with short notes on the multiple elections in 2015 that culminated with the U.D.P.'s historic third-term victory.

The author has systematically examined Belizean newspapers, particularly that goldmine of Belizean history, the *Belize Billboard*, to gather a wide array of information on these parties. The focal points of the narrative are the parties' origins, leaders, candidates, aims, performance in elections, stance on national issues and, all too often, their demise or merger. The numerous tables of elections results are a great resource, as well as Appendix IV with the national elections results (1984-2015). Thus, the book provides a handy guide for the student who perhaps has never heard of the Christian Democratic Party, (nor its predecessor the Democratic Agricultural and Labour Party), nor the People's Democratic Party. The strength of the work lay in the author's unbiased account of the trajectory of these political parties. With such a sturdy foundation, others (in line with the works of Cedric Grant, Assad Shoman, Evan X Hyde, Myrtle Palacio, Nicholas Pollard, Jr., Godfrey Smith, and Dylan Vernon) may wish to probe deeper into the parties' histories and impacts; for example, the chronic failure of third party candidates to make it first past the post in party politics in Belize cries out for analysis.

This substantially revised and expanded Narrative is a testament to the author's persistent dedication since 1987 to ensure that the contributions of all the political parties to

Belize's development will not go unrecognized. It adds to the number of affordable books that are now available to teach Belizean politics at the tertiary level – an undertaking that is too long overdue. Clearly, both the student and general public will remain indebted to the author for deepening our appreciation of the roots of our young but vibrant democracy.

Dr. Herman Byrd

ACKNOWLEDGEMENTS

The researching, writing and eventual publication of this book owes gratitude to several persons and entities. As expressed in the Preface the author spent many long hours gathering data on political parties and personalities as found in the early issues of the *Belize Billboard*, the Daily Clarion, and the Belize Times newspapers. I am grateful that the National Heritage Library of the Belize National Library Service and Information System (BNLSIS), where these newspapers are conserved and preserved, enabled ready access to me. Special mention must be made to Assistant Librarian Michael Bradley through his ability as my research assistant. Every facility was afforded me, and the staff encouragement for me to complete the book was heartening.

Much appreciation must be given to Dr. Herman Byrd of the Belize Archives and Records Service, who readily agreed to read the manuscript and offered valuable inputs as to content and format of the text, as well as writing the Foreword. I am also grateful to Francis Humphreys for assessing the manuscript. Mr. Nigel Encalada of the Institute of Social and Cultural Research provided comments and suggestions on the text, as well as facilitated publication through the National Institute of Culture and History.

An extensive assessment and critique of the manuscript was expertly done by Dr. Dylan Vernon, who also provided me with relevant pictures for inclusion in the book. For this I am most grateful.

My heartfelt thanks to Margaret Reynolds who patiently arranged, formatted, and organized the book to be ready for publication.

My immediate family was always a source of great encouragement and understanding in my completing the work, and I thank them heartily.

PROLOGUE

"I'd rather be a dead hero than a living coward."
[Antonio Soberanis, 1934]

Although in a strict sense the history of Belize's political parties 'officially' dates from 1950, the efforts of one man who defied the colonial masters from the early 1930s can justifiably be said to be the genesis of the nationalist movement.

Born to Mexican parents in the village of San Antonio, Rio Hondo in 1897, Antonio Soberanis Gomez began his career as an activist in Belize's labor movement. A barber by profession, his establishment The Panama Barbershop, originally located on Handyside Street and then Queen Street in Belize City, was the scene of many political discussions. Those early conversations centered mainly on the woeful labor conditions of the day, which prompted Soberanis to take a stand for the unemployed and poor people. Those labor conditions had their roots firstly in the major economic crisis which started in 1929 in North America, called the Great Depression; and secondly a hurricane in 1931 which added physical destruction and social and economic problems to Belize.

The terrible living conditions for the working class was at its height during 1934, and even though the colonial government organized some temporary work programs those only provided limited relief. Anecdotally, people especially in Belize City, suffered from such extreme poverty and near starvation that 'rice lab'[iii] was distributed to the public at the entrance to the Belize City prison.

18

In a further effort to alleviate the unemployment problem, in February of 1934 a group called the "Unemployed Brigade" marched through the streets to Government House and requested of the Governor more work and better pay. The only concession made by the Governor was to offer 80 jobs to an estimated 1,800 unemployed workers to break stones at 25 cents a day on the northern road. Antonio Soberanis was a part of that demonstration, and although the leaders of the "Unemployed Brigade" resigned in frustration he stood firm while uttering the famous declaration that he would prefer to be "*a dead hero than a living coward*".

Antonio Soberanis made his maiden speech on March 16, 1934 on the Battlefield, and over the succeeding months he verbally attacked the rich merchants, the Governor, the magistrate, the police, and the British monarch. Joined by colleagues John Neal, James Barnett, James and Henry Middleton, the Lahoodie brothers, Archibald Lodge, Chano Lovell, Gabriel Adderly, Alfred Hall and Benjamin Reneau, Soberanis formed the "Labor and Unemployed Association" (L. U. A.) in July of 1934.

At 5,000 members strong, the L. U. A. enabled, for the first time in Belize's colonial history, the working class masses to go into open revolt against the colonial government. By September 1934 this group had organized many boycotts, demonstrations and pickets against the Belize Estate and Produce Company (B. E. C.), John Harley and Company, Hofius and Hildebrant, Melhado and Sons, and Brodies. Taking his campaign of work for the unemployed all over the country, in late September 1934 while in Stann Creek, Soberanis succeeded in raising the wages of dock workers loading grapefruit.

Soberanis, who came to be known as the "Father of Belizean Nationalism," preceded and presaged going to jail for his beliefs, as was to occur with Philip Goldson and Leigh Richardson 18 years later. On October 1, 1934 when Soberanis organized a picket of the B. E. C. to convince workers to strike for more pay, the picket turned into a riot and a demonstrator was wounded. Several of the demonstrators were imprisoned, and Soberanis himself was arrested when he went to post bail for them. He was not granted bail for five weeks, and spent that time in jail.

Following Soberanis' stint in jail a split occurred in the L. U. A., and he had to recruit new officers. By this time the colonial powers, under Governor Alan Burns, was agitating strongly for a law to be passed which would curb the speeches of Soberanis. In the Governor's view they were becoming "*more and more offensive and inflammatory*" and were the "*ravings of a semi-lunatic*". The prejudices of the colonials of that period of Belize's history were perhaps best evidenced by the derogatory views expressed by Burns: "*I desire to emphasize the point that while these speeches might do little harm among an intelligent population, they are doing considerable harm in British Honduras.*"

The law that was passed in 1935 basically dealing with Crimes against Public Order and governing Seditious Intention remains in the Laws of Belize today almost word for word. It virtually made any criticism of the Government a seditious act, and was obviously aimed at giving the administration power to retain Soberanis the very next time he spoke in public. Armed then with a powerful piece of legislation, the government lay in wait for him to resume his verbal attacks on those in authority.

That opportunity presented itself on October 1, 1935 when Soberanis spoke in Corozal Town to a crowd of some 250 persons. He castigated almost everyone in power, calling the Belize merchants "bloodsuckers," the Corozal District Commissioner a "mercenary," and the Governor "a damned liar and a crook". He was arrested the following day, and on October 5 was tried and convicted in the Corozal District court of uttering insulting words against various persons and fined $85.00 or serve four and a half months hard labor.

The charge of "bringing His Majesty into contempt" was set for trial in the Supreme Court. Governor Burns, ecstatic over his victory, stated: *"I hope Tony will be put away for a good long sentence and that the Chief Justice does not release him on appeal."*[iii] Burns, however, was not to get his wish, because the Chief Justice dismissed the charge in January 1936. He argued that the Criminal Code Amendment Ordinance of 1935 under which Soberanis had been summarily convicted in Corozal *"goes far beyond the English Law – to make words which may be slanderous a criminal offence"*. The Chief Justice thus reduced the original sentence to $25.00 or one month's hard labor.

Antonio Soberanis who within two years had moved the masses on the Battlefield and stood up for the unemployed and dominated the local news, after 1936 rarely appeared in the newspapers or in the Governor's dispatches. He remains a noteworthy political figure because he attacked the colonial officials and questioned the need for Crown Colony government. Through his short lived L. U. A. he operated a feeding program and a medical wing which later became known as the Black Cross Nurses. By taking the movement into the districts he allowed the entire country to think about the rights of workers.

Antonio Soberanis saw himself as a 'stop-gap' leader who was only filling a slot until a middle-class intellectual could come forward to properly lead the dispossessed masses. His political activities continued up to 1942 when he left to work on the construction of the Panama Canal. He was present, however, when in 1950 the mantle of his movement was passed to the newly formed People's Committee, then to the People's United Party of which he became a councilor.

The great patriot and paver of Belize's nationalist movement, Antonio Soberanis, died on April 14, 1975 at age 78 and buried at his farm in Santana Village. A bust in his honor stands at the Battlefield Park in Belize City.

Figure 1 - Antonio Soberanis

SECTION ONE
EMERGENCE OF THE PEOPLE'S UNITED PARTY

From the People's Committee to Independence

Following a resolution made at the Battlefieldiv in Belize City on the night of December 31, 1949 when the dollar was devalued, a People's Committee (P.C.) came into being and was to be the nucleus of the first organized national political party in Belize. The leaders of the P.C. were:

- John Smith, the Senior Elected Member for the Belize Division in the Legislative Council, who was selected as Chairman.
- George Price, a Councilor in the Belize City Council, who was appointed Secretary.
- Philip Goldson, the Editor of the Belize Billboard, who had recently returned from a journalism course in London and immediately joined in the political fray.

The young and vigorous leaders of the P.C., buoyed by the novelty of political agitation and supported by the masses, had a three-fold objective: (i) dollar back and development, (ii) anti-federation with the West Indies, and (iii) removal of the Governor's reserve powers. The first one had come about with the colonial Governor Sir Ronald Garvey devaluing the Belize dollar. The second was protesting the British desire for Belize to federate which could result in the West Indies becoming one big slave camp. Thirdly, the reserve powers under Clause Six of the constitution had allowed the Governor to exercise this in the devaluation of the dollar.

Beginning from early January 1950 the P.C. held regular meetings at the Battlefield, during which heated speeches expressing the views of the people were delivered. At one of those meetings, on January 10, the people conferred on the P.C. a mandate to approach the United Nations in the cause of the "Dollar Back" fight.

The Flag of the Baymen

Matters were taken a step further on February 1 when the people expressed their desire to be identified as a 'free people' by raising the flag of the Baymen[2] on the Battlefield. While a band played, thousands of people sang "God Bless America," and the flag of the Baymen which up to 70 years before had flown over the Settlement of Belize was hoisted on a flagpole. John Smith was greeted by cheers as he mounted the rostrum and declared:

> *"People of Honduras, we have recovered the ancient flag of our Baymen fathers."*

He was followed by George Price who called attention to the flag by saying:

> *"Behold the ancient flag of this country. Blue as the skies above – high ideals of democracy; the coat of arms – the symbol of our country. Take it, protect it, love it."*

Pointing then to the flagstaff at the Courthouse, amidst loud cheers, he asserted:

---

[2]During the 18th Century several logging camps, comprising of Negroes and Scots, sprang up along the coast from Yucatan to the Republic of Honduras, including the Bay Islands and Nicaragua. The inhabitants of these logging camps became known as Baymen. The Baymen flag is a light blue color. In the center is the coat of arms of the Settlement of Belize on a white circle.

"And perhaps someday if it is your wish, we shall move it from here and put it over there."

Alliance with the General Workers Union

As a means of gaining added strength and recognition the P.C. allied itself with the General Workers Union (G.W.U.),[3] which at that time was the only real organized body fighting the cause of the working class. This alliance would serve to solidify and bolster the popular mass party which later succeeded the P.C.

People Agitation

Heated as the people were after devaluation and feeling at once, with the urging of the P.C., that their cause for greater self-determination was one worth fighting for it was not long before small instances of violence erupted. On midday of February 13, 1950, a crowd attending a P.C. meeting at the Battlefield became infuriated on being informed that certain members of the City Council had voted in favor of having the keys of the City presented to Britain's Princess Alice on her arrival. City Councilor M. B. L. Wilson was physically abused, Councilor Gordon Leacock chased, the office windows of Monrad Metzgen broken, and the home of the Hon. W. H. Courtenay stoned. Fortunately, before any more serious damage was done, Committee Secretary George Price arrived and led the people back to the Battlefield where he succeeded in dispersing them. At an emergency meeting convened that night the Executive Council invoked Public

---

[3]The President of the G.W.U. was Clifford Betson, one of the original members of the P.C.

Safety Regulations, resulting in the Governor declaring a state of emergency and outlawing assemblies of seven or more persons.

Despite this, another incident occurred at a Battlefield meeting on February 14 when the crowd became angry at the Open Forum Chairman E. A. "Kid" Broaster who attempted to dissuade the singing of "God Bless America" on the proposed visit to Belize of Princess Alice. Forced to abandon the rostrum after being stoned, Broaster ran through the crowd and sought refuge in the Antonio Soberanis barber shop on Queen Street. Riot Police that was mobilized to disperse the crowd was stoned with bottles, occasioning Acting Superintendent of Police John Storey to order that a tear gas bomb be thrown into nearby Wickie Wackie Club, the source of the missiles. Storey unconsciously made history that day by allowing the first ever tear gas bomb to be used against any Belize protestors.

On arriving on the scene shortly after, Chairman John Smith urged John Storey to let him address the people in an attempt to have them disperse. Storey refused at first, assuring Smith that the police could handle the situation in their own way. Smith then took a different tact by leading the crowd down Queen Street into Daly Street to address them from the Lizarraga home. He asked them to go home, advocating that when he went to the United Nations to represent them he wanted to prove that the people were peaceful and orderly; and he put the blame squarely on the Police Chief who he said had lost his head and acted irresponsibly. Speaking to the

Governor by telephone shortly after the crowd had dispersed, Smith was assured that the matter would be looked into, as it was the first time the Governor was hearing of it.

Following the invoking of a state of emergency, the Governor had to go a step further and on March 15 placed a total ban on all Battlefield meetings.

For 137 days, up to the repealing of the Public Safety Regulations on July 1, 1950, the voice of the P.C. was silent. During the interim, however, the leaders had not been idle. The *Belize Billboard* continued its unwavering fight against what it called 'colonial injustice'; and George Price had gone to New York to present the people's case before the Human Rights Commission of the United Nations.

Appeal to the United Nations

Price reported on his United Nations visit at a Battlefield meeting on July 28, 1950 stating that after the Human Rights Commission had studied the case it would be presented before relevant committees of the General Assembly. He took the opportunity to stress the objectives and policies of the P.C., stating that it was resolute in its demands that each individual received all that was needed for the common good.[4] Elaborating some more, he said that what the country needed was a government which was soundly established to secure for everyone the goods which the wealth and resources of nature and technical achievement could offer.

---

[4]This in essence was social justice, a principle that the P.C. and its successor would advocate for many decades.

These goods should be sufficient to supply the wants of all, to provide an honest living for all who wanted to work, and to uplift the people to a higher level of prosperity and culture. He reminded the meeting that the P.C. advocated laws to protect the laborer and to guarantee him a minimum wage, and had tried to stress repeatedly three things: (i) the rights of individuals; (ii) the love of neighbor; and (iii) the brotherhood of man. Admittedly, because there existed a few persons in their midst seeking to prevent the determined march of a united people striving for better conditions and self-rule, Price concluded with this telling statement:

> *"As long as evil exist the People's Committee will have to hammer and hammer until they drive the nail home. Beware of a system that blocks the people's progress even though it bears gifts in its hands."*

Call for a Political Party

The P.C. leaders were constant in asserting national consciousness in the minds of the people, reminding them that to advance constitutionally an organized party was needed – a party which could contest elections at both levels leading eventually to a constituted government duly elected by the people. The most strident call came from Leigh Richardson[5] who in August 1950 called for a national party, arguing that in order to be free what was most urgently needed was a political party that would work for eventual self-government. He was not unmindful of the fact that for a political party to achieve anything worthwhile the constitution had to allow for the right climate, so that civil and political

---

[5]Leigh Richardson was a founding member of the P.C. and co-editor, along with Philip Goldson, of the *Belize Billboard*.

freedom could grow and flourish. Richardson was convinced that the only way to create a healthy climate was to create immediately a 'national political front' which would oppose lawfully every individual, every restriction, and every condition that smacked of oppression under the guise of British freedom.

This declaration by Richardson was echoed by the entire P.C. which saw this as the ideal if progress and freedom for the inhabitants of Belize were intended. The proposed party, if it was to be sustained, had to be assured of the people's support, and the party in turn had to work to assure the people that it was sincere and skillful.

September 1950 Occurrences

September 1950 was approaching, and as the people prepared to celebrate their National Day on the 10th,[v] another display of the Baymen flag was done on the night of August 11 when George Price explained the P. C's stand on the September celebrations.

> *"We have a flag, a beautiful flag. It is similar to the United Nations flag – blue and white. Blue like the sky – our lofty democratic ideals, and white like the sea foam – our pure and sole love of country. Since the night of February 1, the flag has flown bravely through rain and shade, through better or worse, from the mast of the Mule Park and on Queen Street. It is your flag. As we celebrate our day, let blue and white be our colors..."*

One week later, at another public meeting, Philip Goldson in referring to taunts, abusive language and lies that were directed at the P.C. on the radio told the people assembled:

"We respect the Englishman's flag, we respect the American flag, but we love our own. We must live for it, suffer for it, and if need be die for it."

At the same meeting George Price informed the crowd that some people were trying to make the September 10 parade to be an exclusively pro-British affair; rather than a celebration to honor the memory of the Baymen who founded Belize City and established a tradition of law and order in this part of Central America. He therefore urged that there should be no address of loyalty to the British King, and non-predominance of the Union Jack.

The P.C. made sure that the September celebration of 1950 was a significant one, as it was marked with a series of unprecedented incidents. It was reported that some 1,800 people marched through the streets in rain, despite police refusal to give permission for a parade under the auspices of the City Council. Boos and shouts greeted the loyalty address; the Governor was roughly and openly opposed; the British National Anthem was not played when he appeared; and "God Bless America" was sung. One positive note was the people marching to the tomb of Simon Lamb[6] and the laying of a wreath by his great grand-nephew Peter Lamb.

The P.C. had its demise on a Friday night, September 29, 1950, to make way for a properly constituted party. It had served its purpose of awakening the people politically and preparing them for greater days ahead.

---

[6]Revered as a patriot, he fought at the Battle of St. George's Caye on September 10, 1798, and was responsible for keeping alive the spirit of September 10th in subsequent years.

The People's United Party

The 'national party' which Leigh Richardson had called for in August 1950 came into being the following month. **September 29, 1950** marked the end of the People's Committee and the formation of a political party, fully constituted, called the People's United Party (P.U.P.). George Price in introducing the party to supporters in the Thistle Hall, opened by saying that a powerful political party would not only be a good thing for Belize, but a very necessary thing. He promised that shortly they would be receiving the constitution of the party, which should be the rallying signal for all citizens to join and work for better conditions. He assured everyone that if they received the constitution with confidence and enthusiasm, and if they enrolled as party members by the thousands, then they would be embarking on the road to political and economic advancement. This would not only result in municipal and national election victories, but in eventually directing and controlling the country's affairs.

The actual constitution, in summary, was then presented to the gathering by Philip Goldson:

- Members may be either registered voters or persons at least 18 years of age with three years residence in Belize.
- The Party would be governed at various levels by district executive committees controlled by a Central Executive Council, which would be under the supreme authority of a Convention of Delegates appointed by members throughout the country.

- Municipal candidates were to be selected by district conventions, while national candidates would be chosen by the Convention of Delegates from among persons proposed by the various district conventions.

John Smith as Party Leader

Registering as the first member of the P.U.P. was John Smith, who also took the pledge as the Party Leader. Other officers of the party were:

George Price	Secretary
Philip Goldson	Assistant Secretary
Leigh Richardson	Chairman
Cameron Gabb	Councilor
Henry Middleton	Councilor

Proudly boasting the slogan: The Only Party, Your Only Hope, the P. U. P established its headquarters on Albert Street adjoining Rita's Store at the corner of Church Street. Before the end of the year branches of the party were formed in the towns of Stann Creek, Corozal and El Cayo.

Seditious Intent Charge

With lofty aims of industrial and agricultural development, adult suffrage, equitable laws and self-government being projected in the columns of the *Belize Billboard* by the very radical editors Goldson and Richardson, it was not long before legal action was taken against the newspaper. Goldson was charged with publishing 'words with seditious intent' to wit:

> *"A letter dispatched to His Excellency the Governor received an evasive reply which could only have originated from a desire to deceive the people of this country."*

Figure 2 - John Smith

Richardson was charged separately with having said 'with seditious intent' at a meeting at the Courthouse Wharf on October 6, 1950, words implying that the Governor was a **"gangster"** and a **"liar or dishonest person"**. Committed to stand trial in the January 1951 sessions of the Supreme Court, Goldson flew to Jamaica to secure the legal assistance of eminent Jamaican solicitor Noel Nethersole. Before

Nethersole could arrive, however, on January 29 the sedition charges against both journalists were withdrawn when they apologetically retracted the charges they had made against the Governor.

The decision to retract their words, although taken by Goldson and Richardson as their personal decision, turned out to be a sensitive matter for the other P. U. P leaders who immediately called a meeting on February 1, 1951 to consider the action of the two newspaper men. The meeting was split and ended in disagreement when members could reach no decision on the 'compromise,' as they called it. George Price termed it a **"dishonorable settlement"** and further moved that the Party record its disagreement with the action. John Smith, on the other hand, completely approved of the action, as did Nethersole in a message a few days later.

City Council Election 1950

The P. U. P contested an election for the first time in its history, when on November 20, 1950 their candidates[7] won a majority of votes in the Belize City Council. Other candidates returned were: the Democratic Party's Lionel Francis, and independents Herbert Fuller, Ebenezer Barrow and Egbert Brackett. Recorded as the largest municipal election ever held in Belize, and proving at the same time how politically agitated the populace had become due to the advent of the P.U.P., statistics showed that out of 2,917 registered voters 1,812 went to the polls.

---

[7]John Smith, George Price, Leigh Richardson, Cameron Gabb, Philip Goldson

Onward to Freedom

"**Judge by the things we have done**" was the challenge Philip Goldson made to a gathering on March 2, 1951, while Leigh Richardson urged that the watchword of the people should be "**Onward to Freedom**". These were in response to the many things the P. U. P had yet to overcome, including the claims of Guatemala and Mexico to Belize, the threat of West Indies Federation, the dangers of immigration, and the stifling grip of England over the country's destiny.

Figure 3 - Philip Goldson   *Figure 4 - Leigh Richardson*

First Party Convention

The P.U.P. held its first convention at Thistle Hall in Belize City on April 30, 1951 when John Smith, then also Mayor of Belize City, was re-elected Party Leader. The original officers were also re-elected to their posts, while additional party councilors elected were Leopold Grinage, Elsa Vasquez, Reginald Bevans and Jose Rivero. In keeping with the party's constitution these officers comprised the Central Party Council, which then replaced the Steering Committee. Resolutions made at the meeting included:

- A scroll be made on which would be inscribed the names of the various P.U.P. committees countrywide.
- A resolution that the British Government should adopt a policy leading to the speedy relinquishment of authority to the freely chosen people of the country.
- The Baymen flag to be the official flag of the country.
- The use of the term 'colony' to be discontinued, the name of the country to be known as Belize, and the inhabitants known as Belizeans.

Dissolution of the City Council

The P.U.P. majority in the City Council gave them the opportunity to be resolute in their quest for radical and just changes. George Price attacked the question of import control at a Council meeting on July 10, 1951, when he said that it had resulted in the scarcity of essential foodstuff and an excessive increase in the cost of living. At that same meeting Price moved an amendment to a resolution that a portrait of the British King be hung in City Hall. He was adamant that such an action should not be considered until the following concessions were made:

- The currency of the country returned to its former value.
- Import controls abolished.
- Conventions of international labor organizations extended to include Belize.

- A democratic constitution liberated the people from colonial rule.

The defeat of the resolution by a vote of three to two in favor of the P.U.P. councilors began a series of events which eventually disrupted the City Council. A few days after the meeting H. W. Beaumont, a retired Postmaster General, circulated a petition requesting the Governor to dissolve the City Council on the grounds that the P.U.P. majority in the Council was being disloyal to the British Royal Family because, firstly, the P.C. had in February 1950 created disorder to prevent Princess Alice from visiting, and secondly, the P.U.P. councilors had now insulted the King.

The matter reached Legislative Council[vi] level, when on August 6, 1951 members voted to ask the Governor to dissolve the City Council due to alleged disloyalty to the Royal Family. The Honorable Herbert Fuller was the member who moved the resolution, which was passed by a five to one vote in favor, with two abstentions. This triggered the P.U.P. the very next day to circulate a petition of its own, calling upon the Governor not to dissolve the City Council, but rather dissolve the Legislative Council. Coupled with this, the P.U.P. made a further bold demand for elections to be held immediately, as the present legislators were already enjoying a prolonged term of two additional years without the consent of the people who had originally elected them.[vii]

This prodigious display in the face of colonial power made the Governor firmly reject the P.U.P. petition, and he retaliated by dissolving the City Council on August 8, 1951. In a radio broadcast, the Governor said in justification:

> *"After my God comes my King. From my youth I have been taught to worship my God and honor my King. As long as I remain Governor of this British colony I will not stand by and see such acts of disloyalty done without my doing something about it. I shall therefore dissolve the City Council, and in due course I will refer the matter back to the electorate."*

In actuality then the Governor took over the City Council, and appointed a nominated body to run it. He appointed a former Acting Colonial Secretary, A. N. Wolffsohn, to be the Chairman, with all other members being either Justices of the Peace or prominent citizens in social life. Two days later, when John Smith returned from representing the country at the Festival of Britain, the Governor in a conciliatory effort offered him a seat on the nominated City Council. In blank refusal, Smith responded in part:

> *"Neither my intelligence nor my integrity would permit me to assist in the retrograde step of replacing a fully elected Council, dissolved for exercising the right to vote, by a fully nominated one. So I must decline."*

Smith, with the backing of his constituents, strongly urged the Governor to put his statements to the proof by holding an election immediately. This was not to come about for another eight months, and in the meantime the dissolution of the Council only served to increase the resolve and strength of the P.U.P. This was especially evidenced in the response and support the Party received as the people prepared to celebrate their National Day on September 10, 1951. Leigh Richardson, writing in the *Belize Billboard*, regretted that again it seemed that there would be a rift in the celebrations because on one side there were people determined to keep Belize as a colony; whereas on the other side there were people equally determined only to bring freedom to their country. Goldson, for his part, at a Battlefield rally on September 7, urged the people to:

> *"Celebrate with the Baymen flag and the Baymen colors, our beloved blue and white, to show that we are dissatisfied with many things in our country."*

On September 10, about 500 citizens cheered John Smith as he reported on the existing conditions and the plans the Party had for the City. After taking a pledge of loyalty to their country, they paraded through the streets waving blue and white Baymen flags.

West Indian Federation

The subject of the colonial government trying to force Belize into a British West Indian Federation continued to irk the P.U.P., and at a meeting on October 2, 1951, John Smith moved a resolution against Federation. Members readily accepted the resolution, and agreed to organize a demonstration; as well as writing to inform all foreign governments, the United Nations, the Pan American Union and the British Colonial Office about the steps that were being taken to federate Belize against the will of the people.

Goldson and Richardson Jailed

The year 1951 was a signal one in the early history of the P.U.P., as two unrelated incidents occurred to put the matter of federation temporarily on hold. The first took place during

October 1951 when the four proprietors of the *Belize Billboard*[8] were charged by Police Superintendent Abraham with publishing words in the newspaper with seditious intent, coming out of:

- A speech made by Leigh Richardson and published in the *Belize Billboard* of June 17, 1951 showing that it was theological teaching to bring democracy to a country by evolution or otherwise.
- An article published on September 2, 1951 reviewing the struggle of the English people against Kingship.
- A speech made by Philip Goldson, and published on October 7, 1951, reviewing the ways of Central American dictators.

As with the earlier sedition charge, which resulted in charges being withdrawn due to retraction, the Jamaican lawyer Noel Nethersole was engaged to defend the accused newspaper proprietors. He arrived in Belize on October 22, 1951, and preliminary hearings commenced that same afternoon. The trial started one week later and ended on November 5. A jury found Philip Goldson, Leigh Richardson and Armando Diaz guilty, and acquitted Lindberg Goldson. The first two were each awarded jail sentences of twelve months with hard labor and a peace bond of $1,000.00. Diaz was fined $120.00 with a peace bond of $1,000.00. Although there was every indication that the publicity of the case enhanced the position of the P.U.P., there were stirrings of another nature which would cause a rift in the Party.

---

[8]Philip Goldson, Leigh Richardson, Lindberg Goldson, and Armando Diaz

First Party Rift

The second significant occurrence of 1951 was fueled by rumors circulating that the P.U.P. was receiving financial aid from Guatemala. This was very likely prompted by what Philip Goldson had on October 5, 1951 reported to the people at a Battlefield meeting on his recent visit to Guatemala.[9] In expressing great praise for conditions in Guatemala as compared to Belize, he stated in summary:

- He had 'escaped' from Belize and breathed the sweet air of freedom for one whole week.
- There was absolutely nothing wrong in anyone going to Guatemala.
- He saw modern toilet facilities in the humblest of homes.
- The labor laws were better than in Belize.
- The effect of freedom on the people and the country could be plainly seen.
- Guatemala was ahead politically, culturally and economically.
- He urged that the 'green curtain' which separated us from our neighbors be parted.

Party Leader John Smith, even with his radical-conservatism since the inception of the P.U.P., was not pleased with the courting of the neighboring country for any financial assistance. Matters came to a head on the night of November 19, 1951, following a policy debate during which Smith's proposals were turned down. As a man who had always

---

[9] *Belize Billboard,* 7 October, 1951

advocated that the chief aim of the Party was to throw off British colonial policies and to lead the people to self-determination, he was also conservative enough to admire some aspects of the British rule. Therefore in his proposal to show some loyalty to the British flag, Smith urged the Party to show in a tangible way its sincerity to the declared policy of the P.U.P., which was to attain self-government within the British Commonwealth. He had further proposed that to give the lie to accusations that the P.U.P. was anti-British and under foreign domination, the British flag should be hoisted alongside the Party's blue and white flag at public meetings.

Resignation of John Smith

Unfortunately, the Party Leader's proposal did not meet with the approval of most other officers and Party members. Two days later, on November 21, 1951 Smith announced his resignation, and in a letter to the Party gave as one reason for resigning the fact that the P.U.P. had been accused of receiving aid from Guatemala, and yet had not seen it fit to vindicate itself. It had apparently seen no need to disprove the allegation either, and under those circumstances he could no longer be associated with it. He concluded that, on a matter of principle, he would not work for Guatemala either directly or indirectly. Joining Smith in resigning from the Party were Mervyn Hulse and Cameron Gabb.

As a postscript to this episode, it is interesting to note that an editorial in the *Belize Billboard* backed the action of John Smith. Party Secretary George Price for his part, in a letter appearing in the December 3, 1951 issue of the paper stated that it contained an inference that the P.U.P. was receiving aid from Guatemala to work against Belize. He asked to be quoted as saying that there were no grounds for such an inference.

In spite of the dramas that unfolded in 1951 the year ended on a note of achievement for the young Party. The people were able to better recognize their present and future plans; there was an awakening to their political responsibility and their economic and social rights; there was a development of their consciousness of the need for a better constitution and better living conditions; and an awareness of the best road to a happy political and economic future.

"Belize for the People"

The year 1952 opened amidst strong rumors that City Council elections would soon be announced, which was a signal for the P.U.P. to start its campaign. It was no longer the only existing party, as a party calling itself the National Party had been formed in August 1951. George Price therefore lost no time, when at a Battlefield meeting in early January 1952, he told the people that the P.U.P. refused to stoop to 'Toadyism. ' A full report of the sedition charges against the owners of the *Belize Billboard* had been sent to the United Nations together with a description of the unsuitable conditions in Belize. In concluding his speech, Price called on the people to use their vote in the 'limited suffrage' to show the world and the United Nations their protest against social conditions and against federation.

In February, at another campaign meeting, there were loud applauses to the announcement that Leigh Richardson and Philip Goldson, although still imprisoned, would be candidates in the municipal elections. Price took the opportunity at this meeting to attempt to dispel the perception that there were ties between Belize and Guatemala, when he declared:

> *"A sign that the P.U.P. is feared by the privileged few, and the colonial working class, is the vicious and violent campaign of lies to smear the P.U.P. as traitors who, they say, would turn this country over to a foreign power."*

He further gave an assurance that the P.U.P. was not backing the claim of Guatemala, and as a matter of fact when the United Kingdom contended that Belize was for the United Kingdom, and Guatemala in the same vein maintained it was for Guatemala, the P.U.P. rose up declaring that Belize was for the people.

It later turned out on nomination day, when the P.U.P. attempted to register Richardson and Goldson they were rejected by the Returning Officer on the legal grounds that they were imprisoned with hard labor for a term exceeding 12 months.[10] This left the P.U.P. with only five candidates: Herman Jex, David Smith, William Coffin, Jose Rivero and George Price.

City Council Election 1952

When election-day came on March 19, 1952, out of a total of 2,955 registered voters only 1,694 persons went to the polls.

---

[10]This was neither true nor justified, since the sentences handed down by the Court had in fact been for 12 months exactly!

45

Although George Price topped the polls, the only other successful candidates for the Party were William Coffin and Jose Rivero. Four National Party candidates won seats: Herbert Fuller, Floss Cassasola, Ebenezer Barrow and Lionel Francis; while the other two seats were won by independent candidates Fred Westby and John Smith.

The new City Council convened its first meeting on March 31 to elect a President and Vice-President. This ended in a deadlock, as did another meeting on April 2. Two days later the Governor, exercising his legal power, nominated Herbert Fuller to be the President. The first business meeting held on April 9 elected Lionel Francis as Vice-President. None of the three P.U.P. councilors accepted appointment on any of the six City Council committees, with Price significantly refusing nomination to the Import Control Advisory Board on the grounds that there was insufficient representation of the people on the Board.

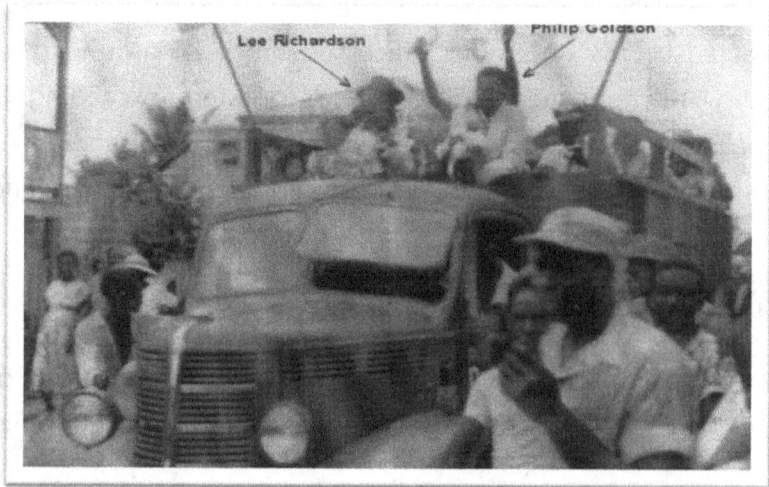

Figure 5 - Richardson & Goldson released from prison.

Goldson and Richardson Released

July 8, 1952 was a day of rejoicing by the people when Philip Goldson was released from Prison after serving only eight months. He attended Mass at Holy Redeemer Cathedral, then took part in a parade held in his honor during which he was hailed as "hero of the day". Addressing the crowd at the Majestic Theatre Yard after the parade, he said that he did not regard his imprisonment as a sacrifice, but as a joy. He had also had the chance to think of new ideas for furthering the struggle and for helping the Party and the Union. Leigh Richardson got the same treatment when he was released a week later.

Draft Constitution

Although a new constitution for Belize did not come into force until 1954, from as early as July 1952 the Legislative Council approved a draft constitution. From the outset the P.U.P. vigorously objected to several clauses in the constitution, and registered their protest in a cable to the Secretary of State. The main objections were:

- The proposal that voters must fill out registration forms before Justices of the Peace, on the grounds that it was impossible for 18,000 potential voters to complete such registration before a mere handful of available Justices of the Peace. It was therefore suggested that enumerators be employed to institute adult suffrage effectively.

- The proposal that the Executive Council[viii] comprise of only four elected members.

47

- The proposal that the Governor retain reserve powers.
- The withholding of adult suffrage in Town Board elections.

The celebration of National Day 1952 was marked by a telegram from the P.U.P., sent through the Acting Governor to the Queen. In it the Party demanded self-determination and independence through a plebiscite as guaranteed to the people by the United Nations Charter. It asked, in essence, that the people be released from the shackles of colonialism. Party Secretary, George Price, who was in the U. S. A. on business, sent a message to be read to the gathering on September 10. He complimented them on having defeated mentally the colonial system of life, beginning to see what was necessary for a free and happy way of life. He praised the courage of those who welcomed imprisonment rather than betray their people and their country. Anticipating an arduous struggle, he asked for God's blessing to make the people:

> *"More determined and more courageous to meet bravely and surmount skillfully and defeat gloriously the forthcoming encounters and obstacles that will come from whence we know not where."*

Dispelling Charges

Although the P.U.P. was allied with the G.W.U. and the *Belize Billboard*, it found that its greatest struggle during this period was to counter charges levied against it by the National Party and its party organ the Daily Clarion. Disparaging comments included:

- The Party represented the minority of the people.
- The leaders were merely seeking personal glory.

- They were tools of Guatemala and Russia.
- The entire movement was Communist.
- The Party was under the Catholic Mission in Belize.
- The leaders were irresponsible.

Allegations like those did not have much effect in belittling the integrity or power of the Party, and 1952 ended with the P.U.P. still on the upward climb.

Constitutional Changes

This was to be a significant year for Belize, in that 1953 saw the beginnings of important constitutional reforms to be effected in the following year. As a result of these preparations, political activity quickened and the people visibly showed an increased awareness of the constitution, and even attempted to assess its possible effectiveness and intentions.

The P.U.P., for its part, had to maintain a forceful front in warding off attacks made by opposing factions. One such instance found Party Secretary Price, at a meeting held at Yarborough in Belize City on January 29, 1953, asserting:

> *"The strategy of our enemies is to smear falsely and propagate that the movement of the P.U.P. for liberation from Colonial evils is wild and irresponsible, and that it advocates violence and bloody revolution. It may be revolutionary in the sense that the P.U.P. is working for a change for better living conditions of the people. By its very nature the Colonial system wielding means of modern warfare makes revolution impossible. It is absurd and untrue to pretend that there are possibilities of revolution."*

49

Anxious to get an early start for the upcoming Legislative Council elections under a new constitution, the P.U.P. began holding meetings in various sections of the City. In a vain effort to prevent the Representation of the People Ordinance in its proposed form from passage by the Legislative Council, the P.U.P. protested certain clauses in the Bill which stated that the people could not wear what they choose on election-day. This was condemned as violating the rights of citizens to vote freely. Another protest was made strongly against all the clauses of the Undesirable Literature Bill calling it a Police State Bill, on the grounds that it prevented people from learning and knowing the truth. Despite the fact that these protests were directed at the Colonial Secretary as well as the elected members of the Legislative Council and backed by a petition signed by 1,250 citizens representing Belize City and Stann Creek, both bills were passed on July 24, 1953.

Leigh Richardson as Party Leader

Since the resignation of John Smith as Party Leader in November 1951, the P.U.P. remained without a leader, until at a convention of the Party held on September 30, 1953 officers were elected to official positions, as follows:

Leigh Richardson	Party Leader
William Coffin	Chairman
Jose Rivero	Vice-Chairman
George Price	Secretary
Philip Goldson	Assistant Secretary
Tharine Rudon	Treasurer
Albert Cattouse	Party Councilor
Nicholas Pollard	Party Councilor

Herman Jex   Party Councilor

Several resolutions were moved by the leaders and accepted by members present, the most important of which were:

- The administration of the country's internal and external affairs should be handled by representatives of the people.
- Universal adult suffrage to be instituted.
- Communism as well as Colonialism to be opposed.
- The establishment of credit unions to be encouraged.
- Equitable land reform and financial assistance afforded to farmers.
- Social security scheme established.
- Racial prejudice, class prejudice and religious dissension to be opposed.

Councilors Pollard and Cattouse had a resolution passed that the P.U.P. offers a reward of $100.00 "to any person or persons or any organization able to prove that any officer or officers have been seeking and/or receiving financial assistance from any foreign country or foreign source with a view to the violent or subversive overthrow of the administration". The reason for moving such a resolution was due to the fact that for three years opponents of the P.U.P. had been asserting, and the Colonial Government itself had been implying, that the P.U.P. received financial assistance from Guatemala. The point here was that so far no proof of this had ever been advanced.

The year ended with a small concession by the Government to a suggestion made from 1952 by the P.U.P. to appoint enumerators to assist the handful of Justices of the Peace to register voters. Even with this addition, closing of registration had to be extended more than once, but which served to accommodate by closing date on December 15, 1953, a total of 20,858 voters.

"Evils of Colonialism"

The year 1954 opened with the P.U.P. asserting its usual stand against Colonialism when Philip Goldson delivered a campaign speech on January 22 at a meeting held near the Pound Yard Bridge in Belize City. Citing the perceived evils of Colonialism, Goldson identified these as: (i) the people lacking a nationality, and (ii) exploitation for the benefit of the ruling power which had left the country's natural resources underdeveloped. He urged the people to vote out the colonialists in the upcoming election, adding that the P.U.P. was the only entity that had so far proved to be capable of leading the people out of Colonialism to freedom and progress. The Party was representative of justice for the worker, the farmer, the businessman, and in general for all the people regardless of creed, color or status. Goldson concluded by stating that the Party was led by Christian leaders with a single-minded devotion to the people's welfare, and with the expectation of a positive outcome of the election there was a strong possibility those leaders would lead the country "out of the gloom onto the threshold of a great opportunity".

General Election Candidates 1954

At a Party convention held on January 28, 1954, candidates contesting the Legislative Assembly election were named. George Price was to contest the Belize North Division, Philip Goldson the Belize South, Leigh Richardson the Belize West, and Herman Jex the Belize Rural. Completing the P.U.P. - G.W.U. platform, the G.W.U. General Council on February 12 named five candidates: Enrique Depaz for Cayo, Jose Chin for Corozal, George Flowers for Orange Walk, John Busano[11] for Stann Creek, and George Gardiner for Toledo.

The Sharpe Inquiry

Amidst the constant charges of Guatemalan relations with Belize, in February 1954 George Price felt compelled to issue a policy statement refuting a report by an English reporter reprinted in the Daily Clarion. The item alleged that a person from Belize residing in Guatemala had made certain statements regarding P.U.P. ties with Guatemala. In denying the allegations, Price affirmed:

> *"These charges are dirty lies. The truth is that the P.U.P. is not turning this country over to Guatemala or any other country. The P.U.P. is vindicating the rights of the people to possess their own land and to rule and govern themselves in the manner that suits their interests best."*

It was not long before those allegations of P.U.P. pro-Guatemalan activities reached the ears of some members of the British House of Commons. In reply to a question from

---

[11]On nomination day John Busano was replaced by Nathaniel Cacho, because Busano had not resided in the country for the time specified to allow him to stand for election.

one member on March 10, 1954, the Undersecretary for Commonwealth Relations replied:

> *"In view of the allegations which have been made from time to time of connections between the P.U.P. and Guatemala, it has been decided that an impartial inquiry shall be held as soon as possible by a commissioner from outside the Colony."*

Because the Party had consistently and vehemently denied that there was any truth in the allegations the decision was taken mildly, prompting Party Leader Richardson to comment that the P.U.P. had absolutely nothing to fear from any inquiry of that sort. What bothered the Party more than anything else was the timing of such an inquiry, which was practically on the eve of the general election slated for April 28. Consequently, Secretary Price hurriedly sent a letter to the Colonial Secretary, along with a telegram for transmission to the Secretary of State for the Colonies, branding an investigation of the P.U.P. on the eve of the election as a political trick. He further requested that if an inquiry was to be held at all, that it be conducted by United States Senator Joseph McCarthy,[12] rather than a British commissioner.

Convinced that there was a tie-up "between the Central American colony's leading political party and the Communists of neighboring Guatemala," Governor Renison proceeded to appoint Sir Reginald Sharpe Q. C. to carry out the inquiry. Sharpe, who arrived in Belize on March 23, 1954 and after listening to seven days of testimony from several people, read the summary of his findings to a packed courtroom.[ix]

---

[12]Senator McCarthy had become known as a great Communist hunter.

Although the findings were not in favor of the P.U.P., yet the thousands assembled outside lifted George Price onto their shoulders amidst the playing of the song Land of the Gods.

Governor Renison held a press conference afterwards, stating that he felt the contact with Guatemala had been proved and it was left to the voters and the world's press to determine what the contact meant. Replying to a question from Philip Goldson as to whether he felt that he could work with a P.U.P. Legislative Assembly majority, the Governor replied: "I think I could depend on the P.U.P. It would be my duty to work together with the P.U.P."

The P.U.P.'s opinion of the outcome of the inquiry was that, in spite of all the persons who testified against the Party including the stooges of Public Relations Officer John Proud, the charges that were being levied against the Party for the past four years were not proven. Singled out for special mention was the testimony of Luke Kemp, a supposedly neutral witness, who said it was impossible for the people of Belize to not have contact with Guatemala, and that John Proud was unreliable and untrustworthy as he had tried to get Kemp to form a political party with John Smith against the P.U.P.

General Election1954

The first general election under semi-universal adult suffrage finally came on April 28, 1954. The majority of voters expressed their trust in the P.U.P., and their contempt for the Sharpe inquiry, by returning eight out of nine P.U.P.

candidates to the Legislative Assembly. The Punta Gorda candidate, George Gardiner, was defeated by Charles Westby. Percentage-wise, 71% of the electorate voted, of which the P.U.P. won 65% of the votes. With the winning of that its first general election, the Party was to go down in history as winning all general elections for the next twenty-five years: 1954 to 1979.

Table 1–Summary of the April 28, 1954 Legislative Assembly Election Results

Parties	Votes	%	Seats
People's United Party	9,461	65.04	8
National Party	3,342	22.98	1
Independents	1,743	11.98	-
Total	**14,546**	**100.00**	**9**

Although buoyed by the victory of winning at the polls, achieving another measure of constitutional advance, and commanding the majority of seats in the Legislative Assembly, the P.U.P. still could not be regarded as completely in charge. One controlling force in the form of the Executive Council limited its power. Composed of the Governor, three officials, and two nominated members, the Constitution stipulated that only four elected members of the Legislative Assembly could sit on the Executive Council.

Membership System of Government

The call for the people to be given additional responsibility in the running of the country's business was made by Leigh Richardson at the yearly Party convention held on September 22, 1954 at Liberty Hall. On being re-elected Party Leader, he appealed for the granting of the ministerial system to the government of Belize. In the same vein he informed that he would be requesting 12 Million Dollars in Colonial Development and Welfare funds for the country's development for the period April 1955 to March 1960. These appeals had the effect of the Secretary of State announcing from London on May 26, 1954, that he was inviting the P.U.P. leaders to discuss plans for Belize's development.

A delegation comprising of the Governor, a nominated member in the Executive Council Salvador Espat, Philip Goldson, Herman Jex and Leigh Richardson departed Belize on October 12, 1954. They returned on November 9 with promises of an initial allocation of 5 Million Dollars for the following three years, and a further measure of constitutional advance. The latter was justified "due to the good co-operation of the majority party in Government". The constitutional concession was that effective January 1, 1955, there would be three Members who would have responsibilities for departments dealing with Natural Resources, Social Services and Public Utilities; and there would also be three Associate Members to share the responsibilities. All this was confirmed at a Legislative Assembly meeting held on December 31, 1954, when the Governor announced that he had invited the unofficial members of his Executive Council to assume responsibilities, as from January 1, 1955, as follows:

Hon. Leigh Richardson	Member for Natural Resources
Hon. Herman Jex	Member for Public Utilities

Hon. Philip Goldson	Member for Social Services
Hon. George Price	Associate Member for Natural Resources
Hon. Salvador Espat	Associate Member for Public Utilities
Hon. J. W. Macmillan	Associate Member for Social Services

The Membership system of government was regarded as semi-ministerial responsibility for the ruling Party, and also a definite step in the right direction leading towards a greater measure of participation in the affairs of the country.

The Blue and White Flag

February 1, 1955 was recognized as Flag Day, and the P.U.P. leaders pledged allegiance to the blue and white flag, referring to it as the "sacred symbol of the people's aspirations for a true and lasting democracy". The Party Leader Richardson stressed that the blue and white flag should eventually fly atop Government buildings countrywide as the dissuasion to Colonialism, which still plagued "life, limbs and property". The time had also come to attract investors in the country, and plans were already underway for investments of some 6 Million Dollars. For his part, George Price reiterated his statement made a few years before about the flag, that when the day came and Belize was completely liberated from Colonialism the blue and white flag would be hoisted on the flagstaff at the Courthouse Wharf.

Greater Membership Responsibility

Ever pressing for a greater measure of responsibilities and authority, the Party Leader in August 1955 approached the Acting Governor on behalf of the elected members of the Executive Council. Under the Membership system Members had no powers to take steps to solve the unemployment problem, necessitating the extension of Members' functions to deal with that pressing situation. In addition, Members needed powers to enable them to undertake social and economic matters on a long-term basis.

The Acting Governor acceded, and made a few changes in the original distribution of departments and subjects among the official and unofficial members of the Executive Council. He proceeded to place Development Concessions, previously the responsibility of the Financial Secretary, under the Member for Natural Resources. Industrial Relations, Labor and Local Government were placed under Philip Goldson as Member for Social Services, who to create complete impartiality had to resign his membership in the G.W.U. and sever all connections with other trade unions. With these changes it was anticipated that it would then be possible to attract potential investors, settle land tenure problems, and eventually establish a development corporation.

National Day 1955

On National Day in September 1955 the Party Leader spoke on the need for the celebrations to be carried on separately, in continued protest against Colonialism. He also felt strongly that there should be a never-ending fight for social, economic and political rights and privileges to be carried on despite criticisms.

Foreign Attention

It appeared that political progress under the P.U.P. since the 1954 elections, bolstered by its performance under the Membership system, was receiving foreign attention. An article in the London Times September 1955 issue stated in part:

> *"The course of political development has run remarkedly (sic) smoothly in British Honduras since the elections of 1954. This has been recognized by the devolution of increased powers upon the elected members of the Executive Council, who are drawn from the P.U.P. This is cause for satisfaction, seeing the anxieties which were felt at the time of the elections."*

It was not only constitutional reasons, however, that was responsible for this smooth progress, but also human reasons:

> *"attributable to the personalities of the leaders involved. The P.U.P. Government has certainly addressed itself courageously to the tasks it has had to tackle, and has exhibited a marked degree of wisdom and restraint which has been fully met by the outgoing Governor."*

Convention Resolution 1955

At a Party convention held at the Riverside Hall in Belize City on October 11, 1955 all the officers were elected to a new term of office. One important aspect of the convention was a unanimous resolution authorizing the leaders to:

- Seek from the British government the sum of 30 Million Dollars to carry out urgent development and reconstruction work.
- Request the immediate granting of the Ministerial system of government to Belize.
- Send a delegation to London to present the case for these matters.

The year 1955 was regarded as a calm but progressive one for the P.U.P. and the country. The greatest achievement was perhaps the unity and dedication with which elected, nominated and official members of government served the people's interest.

City Council Election 1956

In spite of the fact that during 1956 the determination and solidarity which the P.U.P. expressed was no less than it was in the active early days, the year was to signal a pertinent change in direction which was to radically affect the Party's future history.

This was the year when the first municipal election under adult suffrage would be held and campaigning got under way early. On February 24, George Price expressed his conviction and pride in that four years of pulsing political life had allowed the people to "become graduates of the college of politics".

A few days before the election, Party Leader Richardson returned from a Federation Conference in London, which he had attended as an observer. In his report to the Party he stated that Belize should try to steer clear of any form of federation, and if this could not be done, then the country should secure the best possible conditions before making alliances with any other country. In any event, Belize should not completely close the door on a possible union with the West Indies, but should rather wait and see what the future held. Needless to say the tone of those statements were interpreted by certain members of the P.U.P. to be slightly pro-federation, which was most unlike Richardson's initial position on the subject.

The election was on March 19, 1956, and 4,449 voters went to the polls representing 47% of the city's electorate. The P.U.P. won an unprecedented landslide victory over their opponents[13] by getting all six candidates elected. William Coffin topped the polls, and the other successful candidates were George Price, Jose Rivero, Tharine Rudon, Leopold Grinage and Jaime Staines. This victory signified that the people had shown once again their tangible support and devotion to the Party. When the City Council met, George Price was elected President of the Council and Mayor of Belize City. William Coffin was elected Vice-President.

The deserved merits of the P.U.P. were lauded in a *Belize Billboard* March 25, 1956 editorial:

> *"The P.U.P. is the people of the country. Study the P.U.P. and you will see in its members, in its leaders and its candidates, exact reflection of the people of British Honduras. In the P.U.P. you will see mirrored the strength and the weakness*

---

[13]The National Party seated only two out of eight candidates, while one Independent candidate was successful.

of Honduras. Study the P.U.P., and you will see a people's determination and ability to overcome all obstacles to political progress for their country."

When September 10 came around it was the task of George Price as Mayor to read and present the address of loyalty to the Governor. As a matter of record, it was the first instance that that was done by an officer of the P.U.P.

Figure 6 - Nicholas Pollard

Second Party Rift

On September 27, 1956 the second rift in the P.U.P. occurred. The occasion was the Party's annual convention at the Riverside Hall, when Party Chairman William Coffin made a declaration involving Nicholas Pollard:

- On July 6 the General Workers Union suspended its General Secretary, Nicholas Pollard, for financial irregularities.[14]

---

[14]This dispute amongst the leaders of the Union had resulted in Pollard forming a break-away union registered as the Christian Democratic Union.

- On July 7 Pollard began a public campaign of slander against leaders of the P.U.P. (with the exception of George Price and some other Party councilors who he said supported him in his actions).
- During the course of his campaign Pollard had declared many times that his aim was to destroy certain leaders of the P.U.P. and the Union, leaving only "Price for politics and Pollard for unionism". He had been assured of the full support of George Price in achieving that objective.
- Pollard's campaign had resulted in distrust and disunity within the P.U.P., and had allowed informed and well-thinking people to get the impression that the Party was not to be trusted with the destiny of the country. If this was not put in check the country's prospects for obtaining development capital from abroad could be damaged, resulting in a certain neighboring republic being encouraged to press its claim to Belize.

The persons signing the declaration, who were William Coffin, Leigh Richardson, Philip Goldson, Robert Stansmore, Albert Arzu, Elfreda Reyes, Arthur Waite, Magnus Vernon, Herman Jex, Jose Chin, Jaime Staines and Leopold Grinage, also made it clear that they were at that point resigning from the Party.

The meeting became disorderly when Coffin reached that section of the declaration, which as the Belize Times later put it "read a slanderous statement about Christian Democratic Union's General Secretary Nicholas Pollard and Party

Secretary George Price ". Coffin had apparently ignored a point of order moved by Pollard, despite Secretary Price's and the entire meeting's demands that the point of order be considered before Coffin continued his speech. Chaos reigned when the P.U.P. members that had resigned, failing to have the statement properly read due to loud noises, left the meeting in a body amidst booing. Several persons were injured in the melee that ensued, and the Police had to intervene to prevent Richardson from discharging his firearm.

George Price Becomes Party Leader

Order was eventually restored, after which the meeting resumed under the chairmanship of George Price. The convention affirmed, among other things, the Party's determination to achieve self-government and the Party's stand against federation. When it was time to elect new officers at the September 27, 1956 meeting the unanimous results were:

George Price	Party Leader
Edward Austin	Party Secretary
Jose Rivero	Party Chairman
Albert Cattouse	Treasurer
Alfred Bevans	Deputy Chairman
Jose Cleland	Assistant Secretary

With the resignation of Richardson, Goldson and Jex from the Party, the solidarity of the P.U.P. in the Legislative Assembly was now split. Richardson went on to form the Honduran Independence Party (H.I.P.) on October 4, 1956, and several of the former P.U.P. members aligned themselves with him.[x]

Figure 7 - George Price

Among the views that were expressed in the press on the split, the most interesting was perhaps the opinion of a "Special Correspondent" writing in the October 20 issue of the Daily Clarion:

> *"Leigh Richardson, Philip Goldson and others had from the beginning followed an irresponsible and extremist policy of agitation and Utopian promises. With the election of the members to public office, they found themselves up against the true facts of the situation. The decision which they had to make was whether to modify their aims and views of the*

66

facts presented, or whether to continue to demand the impossible so as to secure for themselves the continued support of their followers. Because of their honesty these members modified their demands and tried to work with Government in order to bring about the much needed changes. This, of course, brought them into conflict with the Party's extremists. Since the two factions could not reconcile their different viewpoints, it was an inevitable development that one of them would have to resign from the Party."

General Election 1957

The important party political occurrences in 1956, which resulted in the splitting of the P.U.P. leadership and the formation of the H.I.P., prompted the need for early elections. On January 31, 1957, the Governor therefore dissolved the Legislative Assembly and announced that new elections would be held in March of that year. This was to be conducted under the same constitution of nine elected seats in the 15 seat legislature.

In its election campaign the P.U.P. maintained its old stand against Colonialism and West Indies Federation, and also for the first time sought Belize's recognition on the Central American mainland. The Party allied itself with the Corozal United Party (C.U.P.) and the Christian Democratic Union (C.D.U.), and fielded a formidable slate of candidates:

George Price	Belize North
Albert Cattouse	Belize West
Denbigh Jeffrey	Belize South
Louis Sylvestre	Belize Rural
Enrique Depaz	Cayo District
David McKoy	Stann Creek District

Santiago Ricalde   Corozal District

Victor Orellana   Orange Walk District

Faustino Zuniga   Toledo District

On election-day March 20, 1957, which was the second general election held under universal adult suffrage, the P.U.P. won a clean sweep of all nine elected seats. George Price topped the polls with 1,335 votes, as the Party received just over 61% of the total votes cast. Another feature of the voting was that only 50% of the electorate voted compared with 70% in 1954. An opinion[15] on this situation was expressed in a subsequent publication:

> *"It is clear that Price captured most, but far from all, of the 1954 P.U.P. voters; and it seems likely that Richardson was unable to attract many votes from people who had voted against the P.U.P. in 1954 – perhaps because such voters viewed the election of 1957 as a purely internecine struggle within the P.U.P., or possibly because Price's stigmatizing of Richardson as pro West Indian Federation restrained such voters from voting H.I.P."*

Table 2–Summary of the March 20, 1957 Legislative Assembly Election Results

Parties	Votes	%	Seats
People's United Party	6,876	61.32	9
Honduran Independence Party	2,057	18.34	-
National Party	1,449	12.92	-
Independents	832	7.42	-
Total valid votes	11,214	100.00	9
Invalid votes	420		
Total votes cast	**11,634**		
Registered voters – 22,058		Turnout – 52.7%	

---

[15]D. A. G. Waddell, 1961. *British Honduras: a historical and contemporary survey.*

Following the inaugural meeting of the new Legislative Assembly on April 12, 1957 the Governor announced the names of the unofficial members of the Executive Council, assigning portfolios to Members and Associate Members:

Hon. George Price	Member for Natural Resources
Hon. Louis Sylvestre	Associate Member for Natural Resources
Hon. Albert Cattouse	Member for Social Services
Hon. J. W. Macmillan	Associate Member for Social Services
Hon. Denbigh Jeffery	Member for Public Utilities
Hon. H. T. A. Bowman	Associate Member for Public Utilities

The 8th Annual Convention of the P.U.P. was held on October 1, 1957 at the Riverside Hall in Belize City, when all officers and committee members were re-elected. Among resolutions that were moved and passed was a vote of confidence to George Price and his colleagues. Another resolution supported and empowered a proposed delegation to London in requesting further financial assistance, an advanced constitution, ministerial powers, a fully elected Legislative Assembly and Executive Council, and self-government by an agreed date.

"Lock, Stock and Barrel"

In late October 1957 a six-man delegation comprising of the Governor, the Financial Secretary, H. T. A. Bowman, George

Price, Albert Cattouse and Denbigh Jeffery departed for London. The scheduled talks with the Secretary of State for the Colonies were a sequel to discussions on budgetary matters that were held in London in November 1956, and were mainly concerned with financial and economic topics coming out of the Development Plan and draft 1958 Budget. The opportunity would also be taken to request further constitutional advance for Belize.

However, before the talks could be completed, the Secretary of State had occasion to announce in the House of Commons on November 27 that George Price had been discovered in a conspiracy. This alleged conspiracy involved an agreement with the Guatemalan Foreign Minister in London, Jorge Granados, to take over Belize from the Commonwealth and form some sort of association with Guatemala. Consequently, the Secretary of State informed Price that because of "his lack of good faith" he would not continue the talks. Price, in an effort to save the talks, offered to withdraw from the discussions and have the other members of the delegation carry on. In refusing this request, the Secretary of State was adamant in saying that the Governor and himself had already agreed that the right thing to do was for the delegation to return home to consider the new circumstances, and as soon as possible constitute a new delegation.

In an attempt to outline the circumstances of the 'conspiracy' Denbigh Jeffery cabled home explaining that Granados had offered them all money, to the tune of 16 Million Dollars, to balance the Belize budget and for development. This, however, was contingent on Belize agreeing to become a part of Guatemala. Price, for his part, explained that Granados' offer was purely a 'suggestion' which they were never asked to accept or reject, and one that he himself would have brought to the attention of the Secretary of State. To Price's mind the mission was not a failure, but rather could probably lead to bigger things.

Figure 8 - Albert Cattouse

Members of the delegation returned from London on November 30, and were greeted by many P.U.P. supporters at the airport. Price was presented with bouquets, one of which carried the message WE ARE STILL LOYAL TO YOU, while the people lifted him on their shoulders. In a brief statement Price said:

> *"We were betrayed by the third member[16] of the unofficial delegation. For months there were negotiations going on between the Guatemalan Embassy and the British Foreign Office. The Guatemalan Minister invited us and said he would inform us of a proposal which would be put to the Foreign Office. He did not make a proposal to us. When we heard of the proposal, we pledged to keep silent about it. The thing to do is to stand firm and make sure that if you are going to send another delegation back to London, then send Mr. Cattouse and myself."*

In giving his views on the matter the Governor made a radio broadcast, during which he formally informed the people of the Secretary of State's decision. He said that George Price along with three other unofficial members of the delegation had attended a luncheon in London hosted by the Guatemalan Minister, Jorge Granados. Proposals were made to them which in effect suggested that Belize sever itself from the British Crown and become integrated as an associate state of Guatemala. Price, as the leader of the delegation, had failed to inform the Governor of those proposals; and when he was asked about them by the Secretary of State his reply was that he required more time to think about them before making up his mind. This led the Governor to conclude that "Mr. Price had the intention of trying to play one government off against

---

[16]The reference here was to Hon. Denbigh Jeffery.

the other, and he was prepared in certain eventualities to see the people of this country handed over to the Guatemalan Republic lock, stock and barrel".

Punitive Measures against Price

Punitive measures were invoked against George Price at a Legislative Assembly meeting on December 6, 1957, by revoking his position on the Executive Council on the grounds that his actions were not compatible with his Councilor's oath of loyalty to the Crown. He was replaced as Member for Natural Resources by Enrique Depaz, the P.U.P. representative for the Cayo District. Price's dismissal was of course condemned by the elected Legislative Assembly members, and in anticipation of any uprisings by the people the Frigate H. M. S. Ulster arrived that same afternoon in the Belize harbor with military reinforcements from Jamaica. There were, however, no incidents.

December 6, 1957 turned out to be a full day for the P.U.P., as later that day an emergency meeting of the P.U.P. and the C.D.U. decided to petition the Government for the expulsion of the Hon. Denbigh Jeffery from the Executive Council. This was on the grounds that he no longer enjoyed the confidence of the majority in the Legislative Assembly which had placed him on the Executive Council. Jeffery had previously been expelled from the Party shortly after the delegation returned from London.

In an effort to dispel any doubt of the Party's loyalty to the Crown, Deputy Leader Albert Cattouse moved a resolution at a meeting of the Legislative Assembly on December 27, 1957, reaffirming the Assembly's allegiance to the Crown and rejecting any other government's claim to sovereignty over Belize. The resolution was unanimously approved.

Price's Story

Through all the allegations against him George Price remained as Party Leader and lost little of his popularity with the people. Amidst all the allegations he maintained his innocence, labeling the whole scenario as a Government plot against him. His side of the story centered around the fact that at the outset he had been advised by the Secretary of State to be ready at a moment's notice to discuss the Guatemalan question while in London.

On the voyage by boat to London both Denbigh Jeffery and H. T. A. Bowman had advised him to see Jorge Granados with a view to settling Guatemala's claim to Belize. All four unofficial delegates therefore knew of his intentions, except perhaps Bowman who was out when Price went for the second time to clarify certain points with Granados. They had only been 'informed' by Granados of a proposal to be made to the Foreign Office; and Price had previously made it clear to the Secretary of State that he did not recognize Guatemala's claim to Belize and furthermore did not wish to become a part of Guatemala. Consequently, the alleged proposal by Granados of self-government for Belize within a Central American Federation was a decision only the people could make, and not the London delegation. In the end Price was not in a position to commit to any Guatemalan proposal without consulting with the people and it was for this sole reason – and not because he wanted to sell Belize to Guatemala – that the Secretary of State became displeased.

The Guatemalan side of the story only served to strengthen Price's defense when Jorge Granados, on leaving London for consultations with his government, issued a statement to the British press. He completely exonerated the P.U.P. leader from any kind of action labeled as 'secret intrigue' by over-zealous, too hasty British politicians.

Party and Union Joint Statement

A joint statement issued by the Party Leader and the Executive Councils of the P.U.P. and the Christian Democratic Union, on the results of the London delegation, revealed:

- They regretted and protested the action of the Secretary of State in breaking off talks which was deplorable in view of the urgent financial and constitutional needs of Belize.
- Faith in and loyalty to George Price and Albert Cattouse were reaffirmed as leaders of the P.U.P. and Government of the country.
- They could not find it possible to believe that there were disloyal or clandestine intentions connected with talks with Jorge Granados in London.
- It was their view that Granados told them out of mere courtesy about a proposal he was going to make to the Foreign Secretary.
- The proposal should not be completely ignored, but be made known to the people.

- Their intention in listening, along with all the unofficial members of the delegation, to a proposal of self-government within a Central American Federation and with economic aid was not intended as 'secret intrigue' by Granados or the Belize delegation.
- There was never any intention of transferring the sovereignty of Belize to Guatemala.

As a postscript, George Price signed and sealed to the effect that he did not accept Guatemala's claim to Belize, but rather believed in self-government under the United Nations. He advocated that it was a first principle of British and United Nations justice and freedom that a man had the right to think, listen and to discuss anything not morally wrong.

New London Talks

The very eventful year of 1957 ended with the announcement that a new delegation was to leave for London in early 1958.

The reconstituted delegation consisting of the Governor, the Financial Secretary, Hon. Enrique Depaz, Hon. Albert Cattouse and Hon. Denbigh Jeffery left Belize on January 8, 1958 and commenced talks in London on January 14. Unfortunately the delegation did not achieve the financial success it hoped for; nevertheless the P.U.P. under the leadership of George Price continued to dominate Belize's political life. This was observed even in England as evidenced by a comment about Price in the February 1958 issue of the New Commonwealth:

> *"There is no doubt that he is experiencing his most difficult days as a politician, but those who are hoping for a change*

in heart are likely to be disappointed. Although dropped from the January talks in London, and temporarily in the shadows, Price is still the man who cannot be ignored in British Honduras politics."

More Party Rifts

During March 1958 Price was again to suffer the loss of some of his Party and union associates. Firstly, the *Belize Billboard* published a letter by Hon. Enrique Depaz which stated that among other things he was not satisfied with certain aspects of Party action and policy set by George Price, and as such he was disassociating himself from the P.U.P.

Secondly, this decision by Depaz was hinged on a statement said to have been made by C. D. U's Secretary, Nicholas Pollard, to the effect that he had completely lost confidence in Price. This change of heart by Pollard supposedly came about because of an address which Price was alleged to have delivered favoring a plan for joining Belize with Guatemala. Pollard, who was always a firm advocate of Belize's independence, admitted that he was always in favor of using the Guatemalan situation as a weapon against Britain; but he was never serious about any form of association with another country. He would therefore have to resign unless the P.U.P. Executive declared that neither the Party Leader nor any other member of the Party should air such a matter in public before the Party Council gave its approval. This was seen as an upstart ultimatum which resulted in the expulsion of Pollard from the Party on March 8, 1958, on the grounds that he "released for public information a libelous letter containing damaging and false statements against the Party and its

Leader". Shortly after, Depaz resigned consequently resulting in the P.U.P. losing its majority of one in the Legislative Assembly.

Those losses did not deter Price as he continued his onward struggle, prompting again another subsequent comment:[17]

> *"A man of considerable personal charm, and an effective speaker, his personal magnetism rather than his policies attracted many followers, though the visions he conjured up of a Central American destiny were also not without effect. His uncompromising nature, his rigid Catholicism, the asceticism of his private life, all tended to lead to uncritical and enthusiastic idolization. To a great extent he was assisted by the rudimentary structure of politics...Moreover, the emotional reactions Price produced among his opponents tended to rob the opposition groups of much potential effectiveness by making their outlook essentially anti-Price, and thus predominantly negative."*

George Price and Sedition

Ever since Philip Goldson and Leigh Richardson had been convicted of seditious intention back in 1951, the authorities remained on the alert for any anti-British sentiment coming from the Party. George Price was the next target when, while addressing a political meeting on March 21, 1958 at the Majestic Theater Yard in Belize City, he was alleged to have said that while he and Cattouse were in New York they had observed that toilet paper instead of ticker-tape was dropped on the Queen of England during her visit there. Price was immediately charged with sedition but, following a trial which

---

[17]D. A. G. Waddell, 1961. *British Honduras: a historical and contemporary survey.*

opened in the Supreme Court on April 16, he was acquitted on April 25.

Figure 9 - George Price

Guatemalan Claim

As concern for a solution to the Guatemalan claim to Belize continued to mount, the leaders of the other two political parties[18] existing at the time proposed in a letter to George Price that the three parties combine to discuss the Guatemalan problem with John Profumo, Under-Secretary of State, during his visit to Belize on May 13, 1958. The P.U.P. declined on the grounds that the Guatemalan claim was a dispute between the United Kingdom and Guatemala, and as such should be dealt with by the foreign offices of those

---

[18]Herbert Fuller was the President of the National Party, and Philip Goldson was the Acting Leader of the Honduran Independence Party.

countries. Nevertheless, on the day following the joint talks with Profumo, the P.U.P. sent a separate delegation. Following the conclusion of the talks on May 15 the Executive Council, which included the P.U.P. Deputy Leader and one other P.U.P. member, passed a resolution:

> *"That the people of British Honduras reject entirely and absolutely any pretensions to sovereignty over their territory by Guatemala and on behalf of the people we represent this Council urges Her Majesty's Government vigorously to resist any claims of this sort which are totally repugnant to the people of British Honduras."*

Price continued to consolidate his regional resolve when two months later he asserted that his policy remained one of economic association with Central America, with a view to Belize becoming a sixth state of Central America.

Advocacy for Self-Government

On August 22, 1958 a very tangible demand for self-government was made when a large demonstration of some 5,000 persons from Belize City and the districts took place. The crowd supported the presentation of a memorial, signed by Price and delivered at Government House following a parade through the City, suggesting that Her Majesty's Government had failed to bring about adequate economic development.

A reply to the memorial was received on December 15, 1958 from the Secretary of State who reaffirmed in very general terms Her Majesty's government policy for the political and constitutional development of colonial territories. This policy was to guide the people along the road to self-government within the Commonwealth. So in effect the request was diplomatically turned down, the reasons given being:

- The country would still have to be financially dependent for a time.
- Self-government could only be interpreted as transfer of power to another country, most likely Guatemala, in view of statements made by both Belize and Guatemala.
- Any transfer of that kind would not be in keeping with the resolution of loyalty previously passed by the Legislative Assembly in December of 1957.

City Council Election 1958

During October 1958 the P.U.P. announced its candidates for the upcoming City Council election scheduled for December. They were: Edward Austin, Lucas Marin, Anthony Meighan, Gwendolyn Lizarraga, Fred Westby and George Price. Among several resolutions passed at a Party convention on October 27 were: that the Party continued its struggle to achieve its rightful place within the Central American nations; and that the name of the country be changed from British Honduras to Belize[19] and the capital city be known as Belize City.

The election was held on December 15, 1958. A total of 4,449 votes were cast, which was the highest recorded so far in City Council elections history. 56.9% of the electorate voted, returning five P.U.P. candidates to office. Although still in the majority the P.U.P. lost some ground, and the opposition was quick with the charge that the anti-P.U.P. vote was split due to

---

[19]This was not to occur until 1973.

the presence of independent candidates. At a City Council meeting on December 22, George Price was unanimously elected as President, with Fred Westby as Vice-President.

As the year 1958 closed municipal elections were held throughout the country, with the exception of Stann Creek,[20] and the P.U.P. won majorities on all district Town Boards.

Sir Hilary Blood's Report

Early in 1959 the question of the Guatemalan claim to Belize came up when the Governor, in the Legislative Assembly, introduced a resolution against any association with Guatemala. This was in an attempt to counter the bold and continuous statements of the Guatemalan President[21] regarding 'Belice'. The resolution was carried in spite of quite a few elected members opposing it.

Agitating for better housing and employment, the P.U.P. held a demonstration on April 3, 1959, presenting at the same time to the Governor a memorial addressed to the Secretary of State. The memorial referred to the previous one of August 22, 1958 which had requested self-government and self-determination in accordance with the United Nations Charter.

Ever since an increased measure of constitutional advance was granted in 1954 with the introduction of the Membership system, which was strengthened a bit in 1957, no further

---

[20]Elections to the Stann Creek Town Board were held on December 28, 1959, and resulted in Allan Arthurs, David McKoy and Carlos Nolberto being the three successful candidates out of five.

[21]Ramon Ydigoras Fuentes was President of Guatemala from March 1958 to March 1963.

allowances had been made. So it was that when Constitutional Commissioner, Sir Hilary Blood, arrived in Belize on September 1, 1959 to conduct a review of the 1954 Constitution it was a welcome gesture. The P.U.P. took the opportunity to submit a number of proposals to the Commissioner:

- The introduction of the Ministerial system.
- A fully elected Legislative Assembly of 17 members.
- The governor to be divested of all legislative or administrative powers, and to act solely as the Queen's representative in Belize.
- The government should be under an elected representative.
- There should be no nominated or ex-officio members of the Legislative Assembly.
- Members of the Legislative Assembly should be exempt from prosecution for political opinions, and should not be arraigned in Court without consent of the Assembly.
- A Cabinet should be set up with responsibility for the administration of the country, and be responsible to the Legislative Assembly for all acts of Government.
- The Cabinet should be further empowered to contract loans and request aid for economic development.
- Appointments to the public service should be made by the elected Government.

Commissioner Blood's report was made public on October 23, 1959 with only a few minor constitutional changes. He contended that Belize was not ready for any more changes due to the fact that the Guatemalan claim complicated matters, and the P.U.P. wanting self-government under the United Nations was a danger signal. In any event, Blood's report served as the basis for a constitutional conference in London in 1960, and for reforms that took effect in March 1961.

Figure 10 - Carl Rogers

Carl Rogers joins the P.U.P.

As 1959 drew to a close, the P.U.P. was fortunate to add an important member to its ranks, while increasing the Party's representation on the City Council to six. Carl Rogers, a former Treasurer and elected City Councilor for the National Independence Party (N.I.P.),[22] resigned from that Party because he disagreed with their policy and joined the P.U.P. on November 19, 1959.

---

[22]The National Independence Party was formed on July 1, 1958 through an amalgamation of the Honduran Independence Party and the National Party.

The United Women's Group

The year 1959 also saw a women's arm of the P.U.P., the United Women's Group, created under Gwendolyn Lizarraga to mobilize Belize's women in eradicating poor housing conditions and creating urban development.

Constitutional Advances

Stemming from the report of Sir Hilary Blood, Constitutional Commissioner, talks in London to propose more constitutional advance for Belize were scheduled for February 1960. During the previous month both the P.U.P. and the N.I.P. formed a Working Committee to present a united front at the talks. The talks in London began on February 1, attended by a delegation comprising: George Price and Albert Cattouse of the P.U.P.; Herbert Fuller and Philip Goldson of the N.I.P.; two independents Gilbert Hulse and William Bowman; and the official Government delegation to discuss economic policy and financial aid. The talks ended on February 17 and resulted in several constitutional changes embodying substantial transfers of political power to the people, the more important being:

- The introduction of the Ministerial system, with the majority party leader to be known as First Minister.
- An Executive Council consisting of the Governor as chairman, two official members, the First Minister, and five other ministers elected by the Legislative Assembly from among their members.
- A four year term Legislative Assembly presided over by a Speaker, comprising 18 members elected from

single-member districts, along with five appointed by the Governor and two official members.

- The First Minister to propose names of his Cabinet to the Legislative Assembly.
- The First Minister to allocate, through the Governor, the portfolios of Ministers.

There can be no doubt that those developments took Belize nearer to self-government, thanks to the efforts of the entire delegation. However, in singling out the P.U.P. Leader for special mention, a Belize Times article of January 29, 1960 said this of him:

> *"After some ten years of arduously fighting for the people of this country, after some ten years of hard work uniting the people of this country, and after ten years of removing the many obstacles presented by the Colonial system, the Hon. George Price, Leader 'omnipotent' of Belize Country, has won another great victory – this time that of uniting the voices of their country to seek for self-government and independence."*

The conditions of the new constitution, which was to come into effect in 1961, included in the preamble a section which rejected the Guatemalan claim to Belize; and another significant section which stated that a referendum must be held before there could by any question of Belize joining with any neighboring country. The leaders of both the P.U.P. and the N.I.P. signed to that effect, with Price definitively proclaiming that he wanted Belize to be a bridge between the Commonwealth and Central America.

The granting of greater constitutional powers to the Government heralded what later came to be known as the 'new order'. The people's identity began to assert itself encouraged by slogans and daily reminders projecting national consciousness. The Party Leader remained in the forefront of the charge by maintaining vigorous and visionary declarations, an example of which was in December 1960 when he moved amendments to certain bills concerning the judiciary system proposing that Belize be no longer a town, but a city, and the entire land be no longer a colony, but a country. These terms were intended to reflect the 'new order' and the new pattern of government.

Figure 11 - Gwendolyn Lizarraga

General Election 1961

The dissolution of the Legislative Assembly by the Governor on January 14, 1961, followed by an announcement that general election would be held in early March, was the signal for the P.U.P. to launch a vigorous election campaign. This was done by way of a two-day national convention, which opened at Memorial Park in Belize City on January 27, at which thousands of Party members and supporters greeted the presentation of the candidates for the election:

Carl Rogers	Mesopotamia
Gwendolyn Lizarraga	Pickstock
Albert Cattouse	Collet
Fred Westby	Albert
Alexander Hunter	Fort George
George Price	Freetown
Santiago Ricalde	Corozal North
Jesus Ken	Corozal South
Hector Silva	Cayo North
Santiago Perdomo	Cayo South
Allan Arthurs	Stann Creek Town
David McKoy	Stann Creek Rural
Fred Hunter	Belize Rural North
Louis Sylvestre	Belize Rural South
Samuel Vernon	Toledo South
Faustino Zuniga	Toledo North
Guadalupe Pech	Orange Walk South
Victor Orellana	Orange Walk North

The session was climaxed the following night at the Riverside Hall when officers were elected, and the Party's manifesto adopted. The officers were:

George Price	Party Leader
Albert Cattouse	Deputy Party Leader
Alfred Bevans	Chairman
Ivan Tillett	Deputy Chairman

Anthony Meighan	Secretary
Melvin Ysaguirre	Assistant Secretary

On March 1, 1961 election day, the P.U.P. candidates won all 18 elected seats in the Legislative Assembly under an advanced constitution. Deservedly so this victory was regarded by the P.U.P. as a strong mandate to govern the country for the next four years, encouraged by the fact that that was the second time in succession the Party had won all the elected seats in a general election. Statistically, over 80% of the registered voters went to the polls, and 64.67% of those voted for the P.U.P.

Table 3–Summary of the March 26, 1961 Legislative Assembly Election Results

Parties	Votes	%	Seats
People's United Party	13,975	64.67	18
National Independence Party	5,107	23.63	-
Christian Democratic Party	2,514	11.63	-
Independents	15	0.07	-
Total valid votes	21,611	100.00	18
Invalid votes	422		
Total votes cast	**22,033**		
Registered voters – 27,414		Turnout – 80.4%	

George Price was formally appointed First Minister by the Governor on March 3, and on March 27 Price in turn allocated portfolios to his Cabinet Ministers:

George Price	Finance and Development
Albert Cattouse	Public Works, Power and Communication
Louis Sylvestre	Local Government, Social Welfare & Cooperatives

Alexander Hunter	Natural Resources, Commerce & Industry
Carl Rogers	Labor
J. Wilson Macmillan	Education, Health & Housing

Having been granted a greater degree of power the P.U.P. proceeded with concrete plans for Belize's development. Helped along with this venture by the Party's mouthpiece, the Belize Times,[23] before the year ended much had changed in areas of semantics and political ideas and ideals.

A proposed change in the City Council election voting process was made by President George Price at a Council meeting held on May 23, 1961. The resolution was that Central Government be requested to repeal the existing law of proportional representation and replace it with a system of direct counting of votes as was used in Legislative Assembly elections.

A Mythical Battle

The Battle of St. George's Caye, traditionally celebrated on September 10, received unwarranted attention during 1961 when the Battle was branded as a myth by the P.U.P. Actually from 1958 Guatemalan President Ramon Ydigoras Fuentes had stated that the Battle was a myth. Then in August of 1959 the Belize Times made the same statement. Consequently, to assuage such perceptions, the Legislative Assembly meeting

---

[23]The *Belize Times* is a weekly newspaper which became the official organ of the P.U.P. in 1956 after a split in the Party lost it the support of the *Belize Billboard*, owned by Philip Goldson.

on June 27, 1961 proposed a resolution that September 10 be adopted and declared to be the country's National Day. This was approved by the Executive Council on July 19, 1961.

Border Incident

The year 1962 opened with an unprecedented incident on January 22 at Belize's southern border with Guatemala. The attention of the entire country was engaged when a party of armed Guatemalans, headed by Francisco Sagastume,[xi] hoisted the Guatemalan flag at Pueblo Viejo[24] after tearing down and burning the British Union Jack. Apart from expressions of outrage on the part of Government, opposing party factions took the opportunity to launch attacks on the P.U.P.

A few days after the incident the Leader of the N.I.P., Philip Goldson, wrote to the Mayor of Belize City, George Price, stating that the N.I.P. Executive felt that because of the Guatemalan invasion in the Toledo District public feelings in the capital had been such that the displaying of the Guatemalan national colors[25] in the city's public square was causing growing resentment among the people. Goldson's ultimate request was that the P.U.P. flag be removed from its position in the Market Square and be displayed only at Party meetings.

In replying, George Price reminded the N.I.P. Leader that the flag of the P.U.P. had been flying in the Market Square for

---

[24]Pueblo Viejo is a Maya village in the Toledo District, in southern Belize.
[25]Both the adopted P.U.P. flag and the Guatemalan flag are similar, with blue and white colors.

over nine years and, moreover, had been displayed there with the knowledge and consent of the Belize City Council which owned and controlled the Square. He did not therefore believe that there was a danger of any spontaneous disturbance.

With the Sagastume incident resolved, the Government turned its attention to more pressing matters when in April, 1962 it sent a delegation, led by Price, to London to discuss financial assistance for hurricane reconstruction and rehabilitation.[26] The British Government gave a grant of 16 Million Dollars.

Puerto Rican Talks

An attempt to solve the long standing dispute between Britain and Guatemala over Belize was again made on April 16, 1962. Until then all negotiations between Britain and Guatemala to find a solution to Guatemala's claim to Belize were bilateral negotiations. So when George Price, Albert Cattouse and Louis Sylvestre along with Harrison Courtenay Sr. as the legal advisor, joined delegates from Britain and Guatemala for talks in Puerto Rico it was the first time delegates from Belize were permitted to participate in the Anglo-Guatemalan negotiations. Although the purpose was to seek a solution to the dispute through economic cooperation, and the Economic Commission for Latin America was to facilitate Belize joining the Central American Common Market, not much was accomplished.

---

[26] On October 31, 1961 hurricane Hattie had severely wrecked Belize City and other parts of the country.

"National Day" Celebration

In 1962, the September 10 celebrations again saw a split, whereby a conservative and traditional faction of the community insisted on glorifying the events of the Battle of St. George's Caye and vilified the P.U.P. for not regarding it. The P.U.P., for its part, explained that it was celebrating 'National Day' shadowed by a conjunction of events recalling the indecision and the struggles of the past, the awareness of the present, and with minds turned towards the future of Belize as an aspiring nation. An article in the Belize Times echoed this sentiment:

> *"Today we are celebrating the memory of those glorious events of 1798 which gave us the occasion to observe the tenth of September; but the emphasis of the Twentieth Century celebrations have a new theme, a new angle. Instead of dwelling on the victory of masters and slaves over Spaniards, the idea is to increase our national concepts. We are looking forward to the future, not to the total exclusion of things of the past, but necessarily in keeping up with our gradual evolution to mature thinking."*

City Council Election 1962

City Council election was due to be held on December 12, 1962, and the P.U.P. announced its candidates at a convention held at Riverside Hall on October 31. They were: George Price, Carl Rogers, Fred Westby, James Meighan, Gwendolyn Lizarraga, Anthony Meighan, Lois Encalada, Orlando Lizama, and Vallan Neal. All nine candidates were elected, enabling the P.U.P. to finally realize its ideal of having a P.U.P. City Council working along with a P.U.P. Central Government. Statistics of the election results revealed that 8,774 persons out of a registered total of 12,731 voted. Of the 77,086 votes cast the P.U.P. received 57.9% while the N.I.P. got 42.1%. At the first meeting of the new City Council Fred Westby was elected Mayor, and Anthony Meighan as Deputy Mayor.

A New Constitution...

Self-determination and economic development were always uppermost on the agenda of the P.U.P., and George Price persisted during 1963 in pursuing the plans and visions he had for the future of the country. In May, he asserted publicly:

> *"Our aim is independence and friendship with all Central America, including Guatemala who is our neighbor. We want trade relations with them in the development of the adjoining large Petén region. We are studying the Central American Common Market of which Guatemala is a part; the Economic Commission on Latin America is about to make a study."*

In singling out Petén Price was perhaps astute enough to see that such development in that region would invariably depend on the communication facilities available through Belize. If development of both Belize and Petén could be done concomitantly, then Belize for its part could benefit immensely by having that large area of development nearby.

Price's attention was again diverted, for the time being, in agitating for some more constitutional change to be discussed at an upcoming London conference in July 1963. As Party Leader, Price formally announced his Party's proposals outlining the type of constitution he hoped to negotiate for Belize. These were presented to a special committee appointed to hold public meetings in the Legislative Assembly chambers, the more important being:

- The Governor shall act in accordance with the advice of the Cabinet or a Minister.
- Executive authority to be vested in the Cabinet.
- Ministers directly responsible to the House of Representatives.
- A Prime Minister shall be appointed by the Governor.
- Ministers appointed by the Governor with the advice of the Prime Minister.
- Two ex-officio members of the Executive Council replaced by Ministers.
- The Prime Minister removable by the Governor only through a vote of no confidence passed by the Legislative Assembly.
- A bicameral Legislature consisting of the elected 18 member House of Representatives.
- A Senate with a President to initiate legislation, but with no control over finance.
- A Privy Council to advise the Governor on the exercise of the Royal Prerogative of Mercy in capital cases.
- All matters pertaining to foreign affairs to remain with Her Majesty's Government in the United Kingdom.
- A Public Service Commission appointed biennially by the Governor on the advice of the Prime Minister.
- A Court of Appeals established.
- An Auditor-General appointed.

Happily the Legislative Assembly approved those proposals on June 17, 1963 and in the days following the Party Leader toured all the district towns to apprise the people of the proposals. Price and his delegation[27] left the country for London on June 29, and at the conference which convened from July 10 to 22, the P.U.P. got most of its proposals approved. Viewed as the basis for full internal self-government for Belize, the P.U.P. held a victory rally to celebrate achieving a new constitution.

The Party's 1963 convention on September 27 at the Riverside Hall was an occasion to celebrate the 13th birthday of its existence as well as to mark the achievement of a self-government constitution. Apart from adopting a new motto for the convention: "We join the P.U.P. to give to the nation – not to take away from the nation," resolutions were passed on matters dealing with communism, internal security and national symbols. George Price was re-elected Party Leader, and other elected officers were:

Albert Cattouse	Deputy Leader
Alfred Bevans	Chairman
Ivan Tillett	Deputy Chairman
Anthony Meighan	Secretary
Melvin Ysaguirre	Assistant Secretary
Alexander Hunter	Treasurer
Carl Rogers	Co-Assistant Treasurer
Orlando Lizama	Co-Assistant Treasurer

On United Nations Day, October 24, Price reiterated his dedication to self-determination in accordance with the United Nations Charter when he raised the United Nations

---

[27]Delegation members: Gwendolyn Lizarraga, Carl Rogers, Faustino Zuniga, W. H. Courtenay (Constitutional Adviser), and C. Henville (Legal Adviser).

flag in the Market Square. In briefly addressing the gathering he said that the flag was symbolic of Belize, because the P.U.P. Manifesto stated that the Party would continue to adhere to the principles of the United Nations Charter.[xii]

Town Board Elections

On December 27, 1963, the seven district Town Boards held elections, and of the 4,943 registered voters 4,010 persons voted. The P.U.P. gained victory in five towns: Corozal, San Ignacio, Stann Creek, Monkey River and Punta Gorda, by garnering 53.4% of the total votes. The N.I.P. got 45.9% and won in Orange Walk and Benque Viejo del Carmen.

... Self-Government

History was made in Belize on January 1, 1964 when it became the newest nation in the hemisphere to be granted full internal self-government. This came about after 95 years of Crown Colony rule by Great Britain, and 14 years following the people's desire for self-determination under the P.U.P. Under the new constitution, George Price was sworn in as Premier on January 6 by the Governor at Government House, while Ministers who formed the Cabinet, along with their allocated portfolios,[28] were also sworn in:

Albert Cattouse	Local Government, Social Welfare & Cooperatives
J. Wilson Macmillan	Minister of Education, Health & Housing

---

[28]The British retained Foreign Affairs, National Defense and the Public Service.

Alexander Hunter	Minister of Natural Resources, Commerce & Industry
Carl Rogers	Minister of Internal Affairs & Justice
David McKoy	Labour
Hector Silva	Public Works, Power & Communications

Celebrations were the order of the day, as January 13 was declared a holiday and all over the country festivities were held. At a special sitting of the Legislative Assembly on the same day, Nigel Fisher, Under-Secretary of State for the Colonies, gave an address. He said that Belize was well on its way to independence, and the people should always cherish the fact that they were free from racial strife, and should always remain a "truly united people".

In Fisher's whirlwind tour of the district towns his comments were favorable and commendable to the Government of Belize. In Punta Gorda he told the residents: "You have a good Premier who has gained the friendship and confidence of the United Kingdom Government". In Stann Creek Town he informed the school children that the new constitution would one day be remembered as a most important event in their history, and furthermore they should be aware that no other man in the country had done more to achieve political advance than Premier Price. The San Ignacio people were told: "This is an important week and one which was well earned. This is due to the culture of your leaders and their wisdom during the past years."

Two days later, on January 15, 1964 the P.U.P. held a celebratory meeting at the Majestic Theater Yard at which the Premier and other speakers addressed the gathering. Price reminisced that 14 years ago when the movement of independence started the main desire of the Party was to ensure betterment for all the people. The task was not an easy one because the vested interests in the country tried to keep down the people. He pledged that his Government would do its best to bring a better life for all, and reiterated his call for hard and dedicated work to achieve complete nationhood.

In keeping with proper semantics, demanded by the newly self-governing country, the Belize City Council on February 25 passed a resolution that the official name of the capital city be known as Belize City. Councilor Price, speaking on the motion, explained that such a resolution was intended to clarify any confusion which could arise over the meaning of the District of Belize and the capital Belize City. Consequently, on May 23, 1964 the Legislative Assembly passed a law making the change. At the same time the name El Cayo was changed to San Ignacio, and 'Town' was added after Orange Walk, Corozal and Stann Creek.

In an effort to establish goodwill with Central American countries a delegation comprising George Price, Carl Rogers and Alexander Hunter went on an 18 day tour on March 7, 1964. The opportunity during the visits was also taken to observe the workings of the Central American Common Market. Maintaining the Latin American theme, another delegation visited Mexico on August 7. That one, which lasted nine days, was comprised of George Price, Carl Rogers and Santiago Ricalde.

Figure 12 - Belize gaining self-government, 1964

"We Unite to Build a Nation"

The theme for the upcoming National Day celebrations culminating on September 10, 1964 was "We Unite to Build a Nation". The Premier announced at a Courthouse Plaza meeting on July 28 that Cabinet had decided that Government should sponsor the celebrations, because the P.U.P. government had led the people to self-government and the National Day could well serve as a unifying force toward nation-building. The people's aspirations for sovereignty, unity and identity were best projected in a poem presented on the National Day:

"I see a certain light
Which beckons me
To walk upon a wider stage.
I speak with one voice,
And still I tell you true
There are so many parts to me,
But one voice raised
In perfect harmony...

Things men yearn for, hope for, sigh for;
Things men pray for, live for, die for;
My people now in happy integration,
My people now with fervent concentration,
My people now resolve to build a nation"[29]

The year 1964 closed on a similar note of anticipation with which it opened as the Party launched a series of campaign meetings in the six electoral divisions of Belize City in preparation for the general election to be held in early 1965. Compounding the fact that 1964 was a politically historical one no less a person than the Governor felt compelled to comment that the people were justified in looking back at the past 12 months with satisfaction and gratitude for the many blessings they had received. They had witnessed the development and establishment of friendly relations with neighboring countries, and they had been greatly encouraged by the spirit of genuine goodwill which so many friends had shown them. It was almost certain that those friends had appreciated the way in which the people had reciprocated their interest.

---

[29]Extract from "Epic of Belize" by Ronald Clark.

General Election 1965

A party convention was held at the Riverside Hall on February 11, 1965 at which all officers were re-elected to their positions. The Manifesto for the general election was read to members and was unanimously approved. The Premier's announcement that the election would be on March 1, saw the P.U.P. candidates lined up as follows:

George Price	Freetown
Gwendolyn Lizarraga	Pickstock
Alexander Hunter	Fort George
Fred Westby	Albert
Albert Cattouse	Collet
Carl Rogers	Mesopotamia
Fred Hunter	Belize Rural North
Louis Sylvestre	Belize Rural South
Elito Orbina	Orange Walk North
Guadalupe Pech	Orange Walk South
Santiago Ricalde	Corozal North
Florencio Marin	Corozal South
Hector Silva	Cayo North
Santiago Perdomo	Cayo South
Allan Arthurs	Stann Creek Town
David McKoy	Stann Creek Rural
Samuel Vernon	Toledo North
Charles Martinez, Jr.	Toledo South

On election-day March 1, 16[30] P.U.P. candidates and two N.I.P. candidates were returned to the Legislative Assembly.

---

[30]Fred Westby and Samuel Vernon were defeated.

Table 4–Summary of the March 1, 1965 Legislative Assembly Election Results

Parties	Votes	%	Seats
People's United Party	15,271	57.8	16
National Independence Party	10,407	39.4	2
Independents	753	2.8	-
Total valid votes	26,431	100.00	18
Invalid votes	770		
Total votes cast	**27,201**		
Registered voters – 37,860		Turnout – 69.8%	

At a victory rally the night after the election, George Price and the other successful P.U.P. candidates were given rousing cheers by the crowd gathered in front of the Party Headquarters on Queen Street. Addressing the gathering, Price affirmed that the people had given the Party a strong mandate to lead the country to independence within the Commonwealth; as well as to build a prosperous, happy Christian democratic nation in Central America. The Premier, after being invited by the Governor to form a government, had the Ministers comprising his new Cabinet sworn in on March 5, 1965.

George Price	Finance & Economic Development
Albert Cattouse	Local Government & Social Development
Alexander Hunter	Natural Resources & Trade
Carl Rogers	Internal Affairs & Health
David McKoy	Labour
Hector Silva	Public Utilities & Communications

Gwendolyn Lizarraga[xiii]   Education & Housing

The National Assembly, made up of the House of Representatives[31] and the Senate, met on March 12 and elected a Speaker and Deputy Speaker of the lower house and a President and Vice-President of the upper house. By this action both houses were thus fully constituted, completing the introduction of Belize's new Self-government Constitution. A Seven Year Plan designed to help the country achieve independence through a viable economy, which had been drawn up to coincide with the coming into effect of the new Constitution, was formally implemented.

The Party at 15

September 29, 1965 saw the Party achieving 15 years of existence. At that point it might prove useful to pause a while and assess what progress the Party made since George Price assumed full leadership in 1956:

- Sugar increased from an output of 6,000 tons in 1957 to 55,000 tons in 1965.
- Rice increased from one million to seven million pounds.
- Citrus made significant strides
- Many cooperative societies were formed.
- Reforms were made to the Labor Laws.
- Each village had its own Village Council, and most also had a community center.

---

[31]As from 1965 members to the House of Representatives served for five years, as compared to four years previously.

- Feeder roads linked many villages with the rest of the country.
- High schools were established in each main town.
- Several persons had gone abroad for further education.
- Thousands of acres of land had been given to farmers.
- Electricity supplies in Belize City had been improved, and plants were being set up in the district towns to allow for 24 hours service.
- More clinics were built, as well as a new hospital in Punta Gorda.
- Over $50 million was being invested in the country by private enterprise.

City Council Election 1965

At a Party convention held at the Riverside Hall on November 17, 1965 nine candidates were approved to contest the Belize City Council election on December 14: Fred Westby, Anthony Meighan, James Meighan, Orlando Lizama, Lois Encalada, William Coffin, George Dakers, M. Usher and Homero Escalante. George Price reminded the meeting that the P.U.P. City Council had worked along with the Central Government and together they had accomplished 95% of what the Manifesto had promised. The Party gained complete victory by winning all nine seats. Out of 17,716 registered voters, 10,004 persons voted, and the Party received an aggregate popular vote of 46,647 while the N.I.P. got 39,732.

Christian Democracy

The P.U.P. government was a constant advocate for the ideal state of Belize to be a Christian and democratic one, and this was again brought out strongly in the Premier's New Year message in 1966:

> *"In March of 1965 Belizeans chose Christian Democracy as the best way to happiness and prosperity for the new and independent Belize...We believe in Christian Democracy as the best way of life and we are determined to prove that it can best succeed where other systems have failed and will fail. For our way is 'Christian' in its belief in the supreme value of the individual; it is 'democratic' in its concern for human rights and the rejection of all forms of ungodliness and slavery; and it is 'revolutionary' in the sense that it implies a transformation and a perfection of the social and economic structure not by violence, but by law and order."*

Attempts at Mediation

The year 1966 was also to be remembered as the year when Ambassador Bethuel Webster, a United States lawyer, arrived in Belize on January 16 to mediate in the dispute between the United Kingdom and Guatemala over Belize. While Webster held a series of meetings with political party representatives and other interested parties in an effort to reach an honorable and amicable solution to the long standing question, the Cabinet assured him that the people of Belize did not want to belong to, or be a part of, any other country whatsoever.

In continuing mediation discussions, the Premier led a delegation to New York and London in June of 1966. Returning on June 17 he told the people that the British Government had given a solemn assurance that there was no intention of imposing any solution to the Anglo-Guatemalan dispute that was not acceptable to Belize. It was never suggested or proposed, either in London or New York, that Belize should not be a sovereign and independent nation. A report, made in a Trinidad newspaper during the talks in New York, stating that "Britain wants to quit British Honduras and in effect hand the colony over to Guatemala as soon as possible" was quickly branded as untrue by Price as he had every trust in the United Kingdom Government and in the ability and integrity of the Mediator.

On July 14, 1966 a bye-election was held in Stann Creek Town caused by the death of Richard Castillo, a P.U.P. member of the Town Board. Out of 1,883 registered voters 1,259 voted, resulting in the P.U.P. candidate Carl Ramos losing to the N.I.P. candidate by 100 votes.

The 'People' in the Party

The merits of the P.U.P. continued to be lauded at every opportunity, and no less so on the Party's 16th anniversary on September 29, 1966 in a Belize Times editorial:

> *"Never before in the history of our country has any one organization meant so much to so many people. Never before has one organization received the support, loyalty and affection of so many people. Because the P.U.P. has accepted the rule of democracy and recognized the sacred responsibility of the individual, it has received the backing of all segments of our society. If anybody is to be singled out for praise today on the sixteenth anniversary of the*

*Party formation, it is the ordinary Belizean man and woman
who has (sic) made the P.U.P. what it is; the voters who have
given their support at the polls; and the leaders who have
worked the Manifesto."*

On October 21 the Party officially opened and dedicated its
new headquarters called "Independence Hall," on Queen
Street in Belize City. After formally cutting the blue and white
ribbon across the door, George Price and Carl Rogers
addressed the gathering.

Town Board Elections 1966

The results of Town Board elections held on December 28,
1966 showed that the P.U.P. suffered slight setbacks by
winning majorities in only four towns, compared with five in
1963:

Table 5 – Town Board Elections 1966

Town	P.U.P.	N.I.P.
Corozal Town	7	0
Orange Walk Town	2	5
San Ignacio Town	4	3
Stann Creek Town	1	6
Punta Gorda Town	7	0
Benque Viejo del Carmen Town	6	1
Monkey River Town	7	0

The McGregor Inquiry

The history of the P.U.P. was intertwined with a series of
allegations of ties with Guatemala, actuating among others
the Sharpe Inquiry in 1954 and a conspiracy theory in 1957.
The year 1967 was not much different as allegations went,
except that in that instance it was George Price who acted to

inquire into rumors of his making secret visits to the Guatemalan border. A *Belize Billboard* headline of May 10, 1967 prompted Price to issue a commission to inquire into allegations "that I have been making secret weekly visits to the Gallon Jug area near the Guatemalan border since the month of June 1966, and that in the month of November 1966 I made eighteen trips to the area, crossing the Tower Hill Ferry at the dead of night. Inquiry is also to be made into my movements on the 20th April and 3rd May of this year". Sir Colin McGregor, a retired Jamaican Chief Justice, arrived in Belize on May 29 to conduct the inquiry. The findings were read publicly on June 2, completely exonerating Price of the allegations made against him.

Independence Time Table

Since self-government in 1964 every succeeding year was rife with talk of an early independence for Belize. Although opposition parties expressed adverse and pessimistic views about that, the Premier's government remained optimistic, which perhaps influenced Jean Fox, a journalist from Michigan, to tell the story of Belize in a series of articles. One such article expressed:

> *"Leaders in Belize are charged with good sense...As a colony costing Great Britain approximately $5 million annually, they could have independence tomorrow morning if they wanted it...But in the words of a very wise man, the Premier of the newly emerging country: 'We prepare for independence slowly. When it comes, we want to be able to stand on our own feet economically, financially and emotionally. Belize can be independent whenever it wishes. We are fully aware, however, that political independence without economic*

*stability and without a universal feeling of national
consciousness is empty and undesirable...'"*

The year 1968 opened with the Premier's New Year message forcefully maintaining the momentum of independence: "We go forth with hope and courage. We go forth under the ensign which is raised over the people. An ensign we will need to keep us going onward in the face and fear of obstruction."

Just over two months later, on March 14, at a meeting in Independence Hall, a resolution by the Party Leader calling for the drafting of an Independence Constitution was passed by the Central Party Council of the P.U.P. The resolution centered on the hope that mediation would produce a satisfactory solution to the Anglo-Guatemalan dispute; and that whatever the outcome of mediation the P.U.P. would be guided by the mandate it had received from the people to lead Belize to independence within the Commonwealth. It was envisaged that the drafting of such a constitution would lead to broad bi-partisan agreement on at least the main features to be taken to London for a final conference at which independence, and further assistance from Britain would be determined. This decision was endorsed by P.U.P. supporters at a Courthouse Plaza meeting on March 21, where it was further requested that the National Assembly commence the drafting of the constitution.

The House of Representatives met on March 29 and in reply to a question as to a time table for the attainment of independence the Premier circumspectly responded: "However much our good Belizean people ardently desire independence at an early date it does not seem possible, according to the present time table, that independence will be this year; neither is it possible at this time to fix the date for an independence conference." Although one week later both the House and the Senate passed motions setting up a joint committee to study terms of an independence constitution, it was evident that the Government was aware of certain factors[xiv] that would delay independence for a further thirteen years.

The Webster Proposals

On April 24, 1968 the P.U.P. section of the joint delegation, comprising George Price, Alexander Hunter, Carl Rogers, Santiago Ricalde, Santiago Perdomo and legal advisor Harrison Courtenay Sr., departed for London to receive the proposals of mediator Bethuel Webster. Delivered in the form of a draft Treaty, Webster's proposals would have given Guatemala a large amount of control over the affairs of Belize. The Belize Government was not in agreement with the proposals and the Premier, in a radio broadcast on May 8, announced that following country-wide consultations with the people his Government had notified the United Kingdom of its decision to reject the draft Treaty presented by the Mediator. [Appendix II]

So incompatible were the Webster proposals with the aspirations of the people to achieve full sovereignty that unrest and violence erupted in the streets of Belize. On May 28, 1968 the Secretary of State for Foreign Affairs announced that since the draft Treaty was not acceptable to Belize, it was likewise not acceptable to the British Government.

———————

A bye-election was held in Stann Creek Town on June 1, 1968 with the P.U.P. candidate Carlos Nolberto defeating the N.I.P. candidate Luke Palacio by 156 votes. The P.U.P. viewed this minor victory as "an important indication of the people's continued confidence in the P.U.P".

———————

On the occasion of the Party's 18th birthday on September 29, 1968, the Premier published a message in the Belize Times of that date:

> *"All objective observers will have to admit that the P.U.P. has brought great benefits and progress to Belize. We must keep up our support for this great movement – to lead Belize to independence and prosperity."*

Although independence was again delayed, and there was no solution to the Guatemalan dispute, the people remained resolute in support of the Party's struggle.

City Council Election 1969

A Party convention was held at Independence Hall on March 18, 1969 to select candidates to contest the City Council election. On election-day, April 30, all nine P.U.P. candidates were successful: Brian Chavannes, William Coffin, George Dakers, Iris Gullap, Adolfo Lizarraga, Anthony Meighan, James Rogers, Peter Thomas and James Meighan.

Lord Shepherd's Visit

Increased hope of an early independence came when in October 1969 Lord Shepherd, the Minister of State in the Foreign and Commonwealth Office, visited Belize. Since such visits by officials of that Office to colonial territories normally signaled Britain's intention to grant independence the Premier viewed the moment as significant, and had prior to Lord Shepherd's visit proposed a motion in the House in support of a petition:

> *"The Government of the P.U.P. was a responsible government. It originated from the people, represented the people and had a sacred responsibility to serve the people. In discharge of its responsibility it sought to fulfill its promises made at election time and was, in consequence, determined not only to achieve independence but was also committed to secure proper guarantees of the territorial integrity of the new Central American nation of Belize in the heart of the Caribbean Basin."*

The petition itself reiterated that in 1965 the people of Belize gave overwhelming support for the P.U.P. manifesto which was tangibly displayed at the polls, giving strength to the decision that Belize should become a free, sovereign and independent nation. One of the more salient points brought out in the petition was the need for an efficient, well-armed and well trained Volunteer Guard.

General Election 1969

General election was held on December 5, 1969 with the P.U.P. winning 17 of the 18 contested seats.

Table 6–Summary of the December 5, 1969 House Of Representatives Election Results

Parties	Votes	%	Seats
People's United Party	12,888	58.85	17
National Independence Party/ People's Development Movement	8.910	40.68	1
Independents	102	0.47	-
Total valid votes	21,900	100.00	18
Invalid votes	477		
Total votes cast	**22,377**		
Registered voters – 29,823		Turnout – 75.0%	

Appointed to serve on the Senate by the Governor were: Joseph Gray, James Meighan, Elsa Vasquez, Thomas Salam, Allan Castillo, Simeon Hassock, Ulric Fuller and Adolfo Schofield-Perez. The President was Ewart Francis.

Municipal elections were held on December 29 in seven district towns, resulting in the P.U.P. giving a much better performance than in1966 by winning thirty-five seats to the N.I.P.'s fourteen.

"The Surging Seventies"

Introducing the decade of the 1970s Premier Price, in his New Year message, spoke of the problems and the challenges to be faced in the "surging seventies". For Belize the main challenge was to guarantee the security of an eventual independent country.

The biggest achievement for 1970 was the promise by the Canadian International Development Agency to install a modern sewerage and water system in Belize City. This followed a visit to Canada in September by a delegation comprising George Price, Alexander Hunter and Vernon Courtenay.

On the occasion of the Party's 20th anniversary on September 29, 1970 Carl Rogers, acting as Premier, in an address stated:

> *"Without the support and dedicated effort and prayers of the Belizean people the success of the P.U.P. could not have been achieved. We are grateful for that support as we girth ourselves to face the challenges of our peaceful, constructive Belizean revolution."*

By October 9, 1970 the National Assembly building in Belmopan was completed, and members of the House of Representatives and the Senate held their first meeting in the new capital city on that date.

One of the P.U.P. achievements the Party had boasted about in 1965 was presiding over the shift from forestry to agriculture, and it was adamant in maintaining that position. The year 1971 heralded the 'Belizean Green Revolution,' officially opened by Minister of Agriculture Fred Hunter on March 14 as a campaign for Belize to grow more food.

City Council Election 1971

In the City Council election held on December 8, 1971 the P.U.P. won all nine seats, returning its candidates: James Rogers, Peter Thomas, Brian Chavannes, Iris Gullap, William Coffin, Doyle Prince, George Dakers, Adolfo Lizarraga and Michael Usher. William Coffin was elected Mayor at a meeting held on December 15.

The P.U.P. selected three candidates in January 1972 to contest a bye-election to fill seats made vacant in the Orange Walk Town Board by the resignation of three N.I.P. members. The candidates were Santiago Rosado, Joe Loskot and Fortunato Cervantes, but since no other candidates were nominated by the N.I.P. the Returning Officer on January 18 declared the P.U.P. candidates duly elected

---

In Town Board elections held on December 8, the P.U.P. won six of the seven Town Boards, while the N.I.P. won one. This victory was viewed in the light "that the great majority of the Belizean people are supporting the People's United Party and its program to lead Belize to independence and prosperity".

British Honduras to Belize

From as early as 1951 the P.U.P. encouraged its supporters to oppose all things colonial, including the name 'British Honduras.' Consequently the P.U.P. leaders usually referred to the country as Belize, and attempted through at least two resolutions in 1951 and 1958 to have the name officially changed. A small concession was made in May 1964 when the Legislative Assembly passed a law making the capital city Belize be known as Belize City.

It was therefore a historic moment when on March 16, 1973 the National Assembly approved the third reading of a bill to change the name of the country from British Honduras to Belize, which officially came into effect on June 1, 1973. Significantly, at the first reading of the bill, Premier Price reminded the House of Representatives that the bill was in

116

fulfillment of the manifesto promise made at three successive general elections. The change of name was seen as a conferring of dignity on the people who were no longer subjected citizens, but a people in their own right with their own name and identity: Belizeans.

A resignation from the P.U.P. occurred on November 12, 1973, in the person of the representative for Corozal North Division, Santiago Ricalde.

General Election 1974

The highlight of 1974 was the general election held on October 30. The nominated P.U.P. candidates to contest the election were:

George Price	Freetown
Adolfo Lizarraga	Pickstock
Said Musa	Fort George
Joseph Gray	Albert
Carl Rogers	Mesopotamia
Vernon Courtenay	Collet
Fred Hunter	Belize Rural North
Louis Sylvestre	Belize Rural South
Vilio Marin	Corozal North
Florencio Marin	Corozal South
Elijio Briceno	Orange Walk North
Guadalupe Pech	Orange Walk South
Assad Shoman	Cayo North
Santiago Perdomo	Cayo South
Allan Arthurs	Stann Creek Town
David McKoy	Stann Creek Rural
Thomas Salam	Toledo North

Alejandro Vernon   Toledo South

Of the 18 candidates 6 were unsuccessful: Said Musa, Joseph Gray, Assad Shoman, Allan Arthurs, Thomas Salam and Alejandro Vernon.

Table 7–Summary of the October 30, 1974 House Of Representatives Election Results

Parties	Votes	%	Seats
People's United Party	12,269	52.66	12
United Democratic Party	9,069	38.93	6
Corozal United Front	1,039	4.46	-
United Black Association for Development	89	0.38	-
Independents	832	3.57	-
Total valid votes	23,298	100.00	18
Invalid votes	513		
Total votes cast	**23,811**		
Registered voters – 33,737			Turnout – 70.6%

When the Premier selected his Cabinet the following were named:

George Price	Premier and Finance
Vernon Courtenay	Minister without Portfolio & Ambassador to CARICOM
Fred Hunter	Works
Florencio Marin	Agriculture & Lands
David McKoy	Social Services, Labour & Local Government
Guadalupe Pech	Education & Housing
Santiago Perdomo	Trade, Industry & Consumer Protection

Assad Shoman   Attorney General &
                                Economic Planning
Louis Sylvestre   Power & Communication

Figure 13 - Said Musa

City Council Election 1974

Of the nine candidates that contested the Belize City Council election on December 11, 1974: William Coffin, George Dakers, Jose Encalada, Joe Erales, Alvan Fuller, Iris Gullap, Louis Humphreys, William Musa and Doyle Prince, only Jose Encalada, George Dakers and Alvan Fuller were successful. The United Democratic Party (U.D.P.)[32] won the other six seats.

---

[32]The United Democratic Party was formed in September 1973 out of the People's Development Movement, the National Independence Party and the Liberal Party as a display of unity among parties opposed to the P.U.P.

"25 Years of Struggle and Achievement"

On returning from a Commonwealth Heads of Government meeting held in Kingston, Jamaica, Premier Price reported to a public meeting on May 21, 1975 at the Courthouse Plaza that for the first time in the P.U.P.'s 25 year struggle for independence the Belize Question had received so much support from abroad. The Party's week-long Silver Anniversary celebrations started on September 21 with a series of activities under the theme "25 years of Struggle and Achievement".

United Nations Mission

In October 1975 a mission comprising Assad Shoman, Carl Rogers, Said Musa and opposition member Theodocio Ochoa was established in New York. The mission was justified as:

> "The Belize Government in its continued efforts to bring about a settlement of the unfounded and unjust claim of Guatemala to this country has established a U. N. mission in New York headed by Minister of State Assad Shoman whose job it is to gain support for Belize by internationalizing the issue."

Giving his personal support to the mission Premier Price left for New York on November 4, 1975 and three days later addressed the 4th Committee of the United Nations. Calling in general on the United Nations to support the right of Belize to self-determine its own future, Price received an overwhelming vote from countries in favor of Belize's right to independence and territorial integrity.

The Government's resolve to take the Guatemalan issue to the international community, after years of fruitless negotiations, was hastened when in 1975 the Guatemalan government[33] demanded that Belize give up all lands south of the Monkey River as a means of settling the dispute. The P.U.P. believed that international support would strengthen Belize's position, remind Britain of Belize's insistence in keeping its territory intact, win the support of Latin American countries, and gain U. S. A. support.[xv]

Town Board elections were held on December 22, 1975 and the P.U.P. was victorious in four of the seven municipalities by winning 51% of the votes cast, compared to the U.D.P.'s 39%.

Vernon Courtenay, Minister without Portfolio in the 1974 Cabinet, tendered his resignation as a Minister on December 30, 1975. His reason for resigning was that he was personally involved as a solicitor for two petroleum companies, Ajax and Ariel, both of which had an outstanding legal dispute with the government of Belize. Nevertheless, he pledged his continued faith in the P.U.P.

Crossing the Floor

An unprecedented action in the House of Representatives took place in early 1976, involving the Hon. Vicente Choco, the U.D.P. representative for the Toledo North Division. Previously he had submitted a letter of resignation as a

---

[33]Kjell Eugenio Laugerud Garcia was President of Guatemala from July 1974 to July 1978.

member of the U.D.P. on February 20 stating that "he could no longer support the policies of the U.D.P. since he was treated with contempt by the leadership of that Party and not as a representative of his people". Subsequently, at a sitting of the House of Representatives on March 5, 1976, he crossed the floor and joined the P.U.P. side of the House.

New Officers 1976

The P.U.P. held its National Convention in Belmopan on November 28, 1976 and the following officers were elected:

George Price	Party Leader
Carl Rogers	Deputy Party Leader
Louis Sylvestre	Chairman
David McKoy	First Deputy Chairman
Santiago Perdomo	Second Deputy Chairman
Florencio Marin	Third Deputy Chairman
William Coffin	Treasurer
Joe Erales	Campaign Manager
Leroy Taegar	National Youth Organizer.

Mark Cuellar, a loyal Party member, was in January 1977 appointed P.U.P. Secretary General, and Assistant Editor of the Belize Times.

City Council Election 1977

The nine candidates nominated to contest the Belize City Council election were: Said Musa, George Dakers, Jose Encalada, Alvan Fuller, Leroy Taegar, Signa Yorke, Edwin Flowers, Lois Young and Evan Hyde. On election-day, December 7, 1977, none were successful as 9,448 voters out of a registered 13,948 returned all nine candidates of the U.D.P.

Independence Looming

Hope for an early independence mounted once more when on June 2, 1978 representatives of the Government and the Opposition met in New York City with David Owen, the Secretary of State for Foreign and Commonwealth Affairs. The circumstances and the substance of the discussions were viewed by the P.U.P. as the basis for the independence of Belize; and any delay in attaining independence after an acceptable settlement of the Anglo-Guatemalan dispute was seen as being contrary to the decolonization policy of the United Nations as well as the policy of the United Kingdom.

Town Board Elections 1978

The P.U.P. took a backward step on December 20, 1978 when Town Board elections revealed that 9,026 voters out of 10,136 registered gave the U.D.P. an overall majority of seats.

Cabinet Reshuffling

Some reshuffling in the Cabinet took place in January 1979. With Assad Shoman resigning from Cabinet, his post of Attorney General was assigned to Edwin Flowers. The portfolio of Trade and Industry left vacant by the resignation of Santiago Perdomo was assigned to Guadalupe Pech effective January 15. Eligio Briceno was then appointed to take over Pech's Education portfolio.

Important Resolutions

At a meeting of the Central Party Council on January 17, 1979 two important resolutions were passed:

- "That the guiding principles of the P.U.P. continue to be those of democracy with a mixed economy and that any other principles or systems, be it Communism, Fascism or any kind of dictatorship, have no place in its philosophy or its activities."

- "Requests the Government of Belize, using the authority of modern legal thinking, to persuade the Government of the United Kingdom to spare no effort to obtain a just settlement of the Guatemalan claim to Belize in accordance with the United Nations resolution passed on the 13th day of December 1978."

Those two resolutions were ratified by the National Convention on February 11, 1979. At the same time there were elections to the Central Party Council, and all officers who had been elected at the 1976 National Convention remained in their positions.

General Election 1979

The general election of 1979, which would be the last before independence in 1981, was regarded by the P.U.P. as a sort of referendum on independence. The Opposition U.D.P. was not in favor of going forward without the Guatemalan claim being settled, and so the people's vote in that election would serve as an indicator. A record high of 89.8% of the electorate voted, and by electing 13 P.U.P. candidates to the U.D.P. 5, the preference was clear.

Table 8–Summary of the November 21, 1979 House Of Representatives Election Results

Parties	Votes	%	Seats
People's United Party	23,309	52.44	13
United Democratic Party	21,045	47.35	5
Toledo Progressive Party	96	0.21	-
Total valid votes	44,450	100.00	18
Invalid votes	521		
Total votes cast	**44,971**		
Registered voters – 50,091			Turnout – 89.8%

Senate Appointments

Two new appointments were made during the early months of 1980. The death of Senate President George Dakers on March 26 resulted in William Coffin taking over that position. Senator Norma Fuller resigned from the Senate on May 14 and was replaced by her husband Alvan Fuller.

City Council Election 1980

Belize City Council election was held on December 17, 1980 resulting in a landslide victory of all nine candidates: Dorian Barrow, Alvan Fuller, Gloria McField, Rafael Chavez, Harry Lui, Daniel Meighan, Simeon Sampson, Earl Ferguson and Remijio Montejo. At the inaugural meeting on December 23 Remijio Montejo was elected as Mayor, and Dorian Barrow as Deputy Mayor.

The year 1980 closed on a disastrous note as a fire, on December 22, completely destroyed the building which housed both the P.U.P. headquarters and the Belize Times press.

Independence

Having internationalized the Guatemalan claim and its desire for independence since 1975, the Belize Government had to conform to the United Nations resolution which was adopted in November 1980. The resolution demanded the secure independence of Belize, with all its territory intact, before the next session of the United Nations in 1981. It went on to call on Britain to continue its defense of Belize, and on all countries to come to Belize's assistance. Significantly, 139 countries had voted in favor of the resolution, with 7 abstentions and none against. Guatemala refused to vote.

Now that the time had finally come for the P.U.P. to deliver on its promise made to the people thirty years ago, it had the added burden of achieving that independence with territorial integrity and security. As such it had to perform a delicate three pronged balancing act:

- Britain's full support had to be ensured since their military presence after independence was vital.
- In satisfying the U. S. A., which had finally voted in its favor at the United Nations, Belize had to prove that it was doing everything possible to find a solution to the Guatemalan dispute.

- Belize had to find a way to convince the Guatemalan government to accept a peaceful solution without expecting Belize to give up any land.

Belize went into 1981 still harboring the hope that even if negotiations to end the Guatemalan claim were not successful before independence, then those could continue after independence.

History was made on January 30, 1981 in the House of Representatives when Premier George Price had laid on the table a White Paper containing Government's proposals for the new constitution of Belize on the attainment of independence. The P.U.P. saw this gesture as "The beginning of the crowning glory for him and his 30-year old People's United Party which began its struggle to achieve independence on September 29, 1950". On February 15 a special convention was held at the Agriculture Show grounds in Belmopan, attended by representatives from all over the country, to study in detail the White Paper.

The hope of the Belize Government was that a solution to the Guatemalan claim could be negotiated before independence. Guatemala, in February 1981, did make serious efforts to reach agreement when it dropped its demand for mainland session which it had insisted on for many years. However, an agreement could not be reached because Belize was adamant in refusing to agree to anything that would not give it full sovereignty and territorial integrity.

The Heads of Agreement

In March 1981 Britain, Guatemala and Belize signed the "Heads of Agreement"[xvi] which was rejected by the people of Belize, and resulted in a state of emergency being declared because of open rebellion in the streets. Although the "Heads of Agreement" lapsed before independence on September 21, 1981, Belize entered independence under a state of emergency. In most towns and villages there were flag-raising ceremonies, followed by various levels of celebration.

On Independence Day Belize was admitted as a member of the Commonwealth of Nations, and on September 25 it was admitted into the United Nations and a full member of the Non-Aligned Movement.

Other events occurring in 1981 included:
- The death of former Senator, Idolly Simpson in May; and the death of two-term Minister Albert Cattouse in July.
- At a Belize City Council meeting on December 14 Earl Ferguson was elected Mayor, and Simeon Sampson as Deputy Mayor.
- In Town Board elections on December 16 the P.U.P. held control of three of the six main towns: Orange Walk, Corozal and Punta Gorda.

SECTION TWO
EMERGENCE OF OPPOSITION PARTIES

The National Party, the Honduran Independence Party, the National Independence Party, the Democratic Agricultural and Labour Party, the People's Independent Party, the United Black Association for Development, the People's Development Movement.

The National Party – 1951

The National Party was formed by citizens of Belize who were loyal to the policies of colonialism, and especially opposed to the anti-colonialist movement propagated by the People's United Party (P.U.P.).[34] At its inaugural meeting held on August 21, 1951 at the premises of Metzgen and Matthews on North Front Street, Belize City, and chaired by Herbert Fuller, Monrad Metzgen opened the meeting by saying that it was the culmination of several smaller meetings held in the past months among certain persons who had seen the need for proper political organization. Following the presentation of the proposed constitution by Ebenezer Barrow, the meeting agreed to a proposal to form a Party called the National Party (N.P.). The objectives were to:

- Secure and extend the liberties, protect the interests and develop the national life and prosperity of the people by all constitutional means.
- Work for and promote political, economic, social and cultural progress.

---

[34]Formed one year earlier, in 1950

129

- Develop the political life of the citizenry by guiding, informing and expressing public opinion through public meetings and Party literature.
- Identify and support Party members for elections.
- Secure the development of a planned policy for the social and economic future of Belize.

Officers of the Party were:

W. H. Courtenay	President
Herbert Fuller	Vice-President
Ebenezer O. Barrow	Secretary
Edward A. Laing	Assistant Secretary
Monrad S. Metzgen	Treasurer
C. M. Staine	Committee Member
Manfred B. Wilson	Committee Member
N. M. Tennyson	Committee Member
F. D. Westby	Committee Member

Other citizens who were listed as attending the meeting included: Robert Reneau, H. W. Beaumont, Norman Lainfiesta, Philip Hall, Reginald Pratt and Edward Pitts.

Viewed as "the answer to the challenge of the times" the N.P. held regular meetings, and membership grew slowly but steadily. On October 18, 1951 about 150 members and friends attended a rally to hear an address by President W. H. Courtenay on his return from a tour of the United Kingdom and Europe. He congratulated the Party on the strides it had made since its formation, and appealed to members to give it every support for the general good of the country. Beginning from October 30 members were informed, through a series of talks, of the progress of the Constitutional Reform Commission.

Policies

The policy and program of the N.P., as outlined by the Executive Committee at a general meeting in January 1952, were unanimously approved by Party members. In summary, the basic points were:

- Constitutional: Self-government within the British Commonwealth.
- Economic: Self-sufficiency in basic food production; development of local industries; expansion of exports; financial independence.
- Social: Improvement and extension of medical and health services; increase of educational facilities; better housing; social security implementation.
- Labor: Improvement of living standards of workers and employers; unemployment insurance.

Announcing its intention to contest the upcoming City Council election, the N.P. presented seven candidates: Ebenezer Barrow, Egbert Brackett, Herbert Fuller, Lionel Francis, M. B. L. Wilson, Henry Middleton and Floss Cassasola. The manifesto promised:

- To do practical work and eliminate "playing of politics" at taxpayers' expense.
- Construction and repairing of streets.
- New areas for building of houses and fostering a building scheme.
- Better water distribution.

- To encourage and promote every advancement for Belize City.

On election-day, March 19, 1952 the N.P. won four of the nine City Council seats: Herbert Fuller, Floss Cassasola,[35] Ebenezer Barrow and Lionel Francis. Party President Courtenay commented on the results:

> *"The working of the democratic process has resulted in a victory for the National Party. The people of Belize, by their free and unfettered will, have elected to office as members of the Belize City Council a majority of candidates of the National Party. That is democracy. Let us all together – N.P. s, P.U.P. s and Independents – join hands together and shoulder to shoulder work hard for our fair city and our people's advancement. That is the only pledge the only promise which the National Party makes and by God's grace will keep."*

After two attempts to elect a City Council President failed, the Governor appointed Herbert Fuller on April 4, 1952 as President. Lionel Francis was elected Vice-President at a meeting on April 9.

By the time the N.P. held its first annual meeting on July 22, 1952 in St. Mary's Hall its membership had grown to 345. Officers elected were:

W. H. Courtenay	President
Herbert Fuller	Vice-President
Ebenezer Barrow	Secretary
Monrad Metzgen	Assistant Secretary
Violet Logan	Committee Member
Seymour Vernon	Committee Member

---

[35]Floss Cassasola was the first female in Belize to be elected to the Belize City Council.

George Gabb	Committee Member
Crispin Jeffries	Committee Member
Irvin Robinson	Committee Member
Vivian Seay	Committee Member
Norman Lainfiesta	Committee Member

The Party's Annual General Meeting held on March 3, 1953 elected:

W. H. Courtenay	President
Herbert Fuller	Vice-President
H. W. Beaumont	Vice-President
Vivian Seay	Vice-President
Lionel Francis	Chairman
Eric Eusey	Vice-Chairman
Ebenezer Barrow	Secretary
Seymour Vernon	Assistant Secretary
Monrad Metzgen	Treasurer

The N.P. had the opportunity at a meeting on April 23, 1953 to discuss in detail the water situation in Belize City. Taking a serious view of the problem the Party's Executive was charged with the task "to go into the matter thoroughly, immediately, with a view to making such recommendations to the authorities as may help to find a solution to the problem".

For the reminder of the year the Party continued to hold regular indoor meetings.

General Election 1954

The N.P. was about to contest its first general election, and held its first open-year campaign meeting on January 28,

1954 at the corner of Cemetery Road and Amara Avenue. Branston Clark presided, and the principal speaker was C. M. Staine. Candidates selected to contest the election were:

Herbert Fuller	Belize South
Lionel Francis	Belize West
Manfred Wilson	Belize Rural
S. A. Mckinstry	Cayo
W. A. George	Orange Walk
C. J. Benguche	Stann Creek
Charles. Westby	Toledo

Election-day was April 28, 1954 and the Party was only able to win the Toledo seat, while the P.U.P. won the other eight seats.

The year 1955 was a rather quiet one politically, and the N.P. mostly observed the course of political development under the ruling P.U.P. since the 1954 election.

City Council Election 1956

Under Herbert Fuller, to whom W. H. Courtenay had relinquished leadership by 1956, the N.P. opened the City Council election campaign as reported in the February 21, 1956 issue of the Daily Clarion:

> *"The first shots in the 1956 Belize City Council election campaign were fired by the National Party in the Yarborough area last night. The opening attacks against the 'enemy' were made by Mr. Ethelbert (Kid) Broaster and Mr. Wilfred Leslie, and the main attack came from Mr. Herbert C. Fuller, National Party Leader."*

Using the unemployment situation as the main issue, the N.P. candidates were: Herbert Fuller, Lionel Francis, Manfred Wilson, Robert Reneau, Floss Cassasola, George Quinto, Samuel McKesey and Roy Belisle. On election-day, March 19, 1956 the only successful candidates for the N.P. were Herbert Fuller and Floss Cassasola. The P.U.P. won six seats and an independent candidate won one.

Merger Rumors

Following the split in the P.U.P. in October 1956, when Richardson formed the H.I.P. during that same month, there were rumors circulating suggesting that there might be a merger between either the N.P. and the P.U.P., or the H.I.P. and the N.P.[36] So that when an article appeared in the *Belize Billboard* of October 12, 1956 under the caption "Fuller not asked to join H.I.P". the N.P. released a public statement in response. The release stated that apart from that being an unfounded rumor, it was also designed to mislead the electorate. Furthermore, the N.P. had remained firm to its policy since its inception, and there had never been any division among members regarding it. The party was not prepared to waver in any direction from its policy and program first adopted in 1952 since it was fully convinced that it had the best goals for the country.

The N.P. came under severe criticism by a political observer writing in the Daily Clarion of October 25, 1956, who saw the political situation in Belize as needing a political party which

---

[36]The latter was most likely and did eventually occur only two years later when they merged to form the National Independence Party in 1958.

was truly representative of the country. The writer felt that neither the P.U.P. nor the N.P. was serving the interests of the people:

> *"The National Party is by its very nature negative. The Party can be said to have been formed to oppose the P.U.P. Its opposition has neither been constructive nor effective. Patriotism is an admirable quality in political life, but it must not be confused with flag waving, band beating, and empty servile protestations of loyalty. A party can oppose the Government in its policies, which may be considered to be not in the best interest of the country, without being unpatriotic or disloyal. An effective National Party should have been able to give leadership to the people; instead the P.U.P. was allowed to dominate the situation much to our detriment and the resulting situation we are now in. The National Party has failed to reflect the hopes and aspirations of the people and has consistently failed to show the dynamism necessary for the political progress of the country at this stage of its development."*

At the Party's Annual General Meeting held in Liberty Hall on November 15, 1956 President Herbert Fuller reported that there had been a considerable increase in membership. Officers elected were:

Herbert Fuller	President
Lionel Francis	1st Vice-President
E. A. Goff	2nd Vice-President
Crispin Jeffries	3rd Vice-President
Henry Middleton	Chairman
L. Burns	Secretary
(Mrs.) C. Dunn	Assistant Secretary
N. Tennyson	Treasurer
E. Eusey	Committee member
H. W. Beaumont	Committee member

(Mrs.) M. Brackett	Committee member
Vivian Seay	Committee member
Floss Cassasola	Committee member

General Election 1957

The year 1957 opened on a note of vigorous campaigning by the N.P. in preparation for general elections scheduled for March. Herbert Fuller was most forceful when at a Liberty Hall meeting on January 17 he declared:

> *"The people of British Honduras have seen the administration they wanted and it has not come up to their expectation. We are the ones with our experience to show them how to do it, and we are going to do it. 'Sweep Them Out' is our slogan for this campaign."*

Six N.P. candidates were announced in February:

Herbert Fuller	Belize South
Lionel Francis	Belize West
L. T. Burns	Belize Rural
H. A. Musa	Cayo
B. A. Avilez	Toledo
W. A. George	Orange Walk

On election-day, March 20, 1957 the N.P. got 4,338 votes, against the P.U.P.'s 6,878 to give the P.U.P. a clean sweep of the polls.

The 1956 speculation of a possible merger of the N.P. and the H.I.P. became more widespread during May 1958 when the two parties began holding joint meetings to discuss the matter. The following month a resolution was moved by A. B. Clark at a special general meeting of the N.P. held in Liberty

Hall on June 26, 1958. The resolution was that the "National Party and the Honduran Independence Party should both dissolve themselves to make way for a new political party". Ninety-seven members voted in favor and one against, resulting in the termination of the National Party after seven years of existence. A further resolution was approved stipulating that the assets of the N.P. be donated to the new party as a gesture of love for the country.

In retrospect observers felt that the National Party was weak from the outset and offered no real constructive opposition to the P.U.P. At a time when most countries were battling colonialism it was difficult for a party, which drew its membership from among elite merchants and colonial supporters who were against change, to attempt to gain favor with a Belizean people bent on self-determination.

The Honduran Independence Party – 1956

The resignation of Leigh Richardson and other officials and members from the P.U.P. on September 27, 1956 prompted the formation of a new political party. On October 4, 1956 the Honduran Independence Party (H.I.P.), comprised essentially of ex-P.U.P. members, officially came into existence. In his inaugural address Richardson said that it was necessary to found a party which consisted of stable and informed persons who would not surrender their reason to demagoguery, expediency and threats. The aim of the Party was not to oppose those people who disagreed with its official policy, but rather to give Belize a sound government. The Party would not enact class legislation, would not engage in any class struggle, nor seek to set up a dictatorship. In conclusion he emphasized that the H.I.P. stood firmly on the side of freedom and democracy, reason and integrity. Aims of the Party included:

- To seek self-government within the Commonwealth by 1966.
- To ensure for all citizens the highest standards of living through training and opportunity.
- To cooperate with management and labor for the betterment of Belize.

Charter members of the Party met at the Riverside Hall on October 11, 1956 to adopt its constitution drawn up by a committee, and which was passed with minor alterations. In addressing the meeting Richardson felt that if Belize failed to cooperate with the West Indies it could well employ measures that would ruin Belize financially and hamper economic growth. As for the actual Party's attitude he said that because it was in its infancy, and prone to large hostile forces, it would be necessary for the H.I.P. to show great moral and physical courage.

The National Executive Committee of the Party, on October 15, elected its officers:

Leigh Richardson	Party Leader
Philip Goldson	Deputy Party Leader
Lloyd Coffin	Chairman
Frank Tench	Vice-Chairman

Other persons who joined the H.I.P. in its early days were: Elfreda Reyes, Muriel Bevans, Stephanie Jones, Jaime Staines,

Robert Stansmore, Terrence Keating, Herman Jex, Carl Rogers, Michael Nembhard, Lloyd Griffith, Charles Lewis, McKay Olivera, Arthur Waite, Dennis Davis, Magnus Vernon and Richard Felix.

General Election 1957

Early in 1957 the National Executive of the H.I.P. accepted nominations for candidates to contest the general election to be held in March. These were selected from divisional parties in Belize City and the district towns:

Leigh Richardson	Belize West
Philip Goldson	Belize South
Jaime Staines	Belize North
Herman Jex	Belize Rural
George Flowers	Orange Walk
Jose Chin	Corozal
Eduardo Espat	Cayo
Charles Westby	Toledo

Several of the members of the H.I.P. had the advantage of being frontline P.U.P. executive years before the split so that prior to the election when the H.I.P. published a handbook entitled "Design for Democracy," relating to the activities of Government during the previous three years and a forecast for the following three years, some political accuracy was expected. Unfortunately, on election-day, March 20, 1957 the H.I.P. suffered total defeat when the P.U.P. captured all nine seats. Out of a total of 11,635 votes cast the H.I.P. received 2,057.

Two days after the election the National Executive made a resolution to start preparing from then for the next general election. The Party felt that the poor showing at the polls was because the leaders of the Party who were Members in the government[37] had been handicapped as they had to work up to the day before the election, and "were unable to cope with the great amount of lies and slanders spread by George Price and Nicholas Pollard among the people". They were now free, however, so the work of educating the people politically would begin.

Figure 14 - Herman Jex

At the first general meeting since the election in 1957, held at Liberty Hall on April 1, Party Leader Richardson said he was convinced that the 11,000 persons who had not voted[38] would constitute a reservoir of defeat for the P.U.P. in the 1960

---

[37]Leigh Richardson, Philip Goldson and Herman Jex had been appointed unofficial members of the Executive Council with portfolio responsibilities as from January 1, 1955.
[38]Only 50% of the electorate voted in the 1957 general election, compared to 70% in 1954.

election. He added that the H.I.P. would work to ensure that the P.U.P. stayed in line and did not create chaos. Later in April 1957 the Party announced that it was planning a series of indoor and outdoor meetings as part of the educational and organizational drive to carry out its pledge to produce an effective opposition to the Government.

The H.I.P. Dissolved

Less than two years into its existence the H.I.P. died. Four months prior to this, on February 21, 1958 Leigh Richardson relinquished his post as Party Leader and departed to take up residence in Trinidad. Before he left he said he was sure that the Party would continue "to appeal to the more realistic section of the electorate and serve as a rallying point for those who do not favor the irresponsible conduct of affairs of government and legislation". He assured members of his continued support and he would contribute indirectly to the Party's existence and growth.

With Philip Goldson acting as Party Leader an advocating for the identification of the H.I.P. flag was made on April 11, 1958 by retired District Commissioner James Meighan in his political debut. In his speech he said that the Party should request the right to fly the flag at Market Square in Belize City.

Following a joint H.I.P. - N.P. Unity Committee recommendation for the dissolution of the H.I.P. with a view to forming one political party under a new name, the H.I.P. voted on June 25, 1958 to dissolve itself. The merger of the H.I.P. and the N.P., two short-lived parties formed to oppose the P.U.P., resulted in the formation of the National Independence Party.

Figure 15 - Herbert Fuller

The National Independence Party – 1958

On July 1, 1958 hundreds of persons in Belize City braved heavy rains to attend the inaugural meeting of the National Independence Party (N.I.P.) held in the Riverside Hall. Chaired by James Meighan, the meeting elected the Party's executive:

Herbert Fuller	Party Leader
James Meighan	Deputy Leader
Jaime Staines	Chairman
Robert Reneau	Deputy Chairman
Philip Goldson	Secretary
Jeanette Buller	Assistant Secretary
Carl Rogers	Treasurer
Lindsay Burns	National Organizer

At this period of Belize's political development it was surmised that the opposition politicians and leaders had begun to strive towards higher levels of political thought and action, and in their upward climb they would take Belize to prosperity and national dignity. It was further felt that Herbert Fuller's stability, experience and seniority in the country's political affairs, backed by an aggressive and strong executive, would counterbalance the more 'chaotic' and 'destructive' policy and politics of the P.U.P. Leader.

Herbert Fuller as Party Leader

Matters moved at a fast pace when in July1958 some key issues were addressed:

- At the N.I.P.'s first executive committee meeting on July 4 two committees were appointed: Labor Affairs and Town Planning and Water.
- The matter of unemployment was given attention at a Liberty Hall meeting on July 30 when unemployed persons gave the N.I.P. a mandate to approach Government in an effort to relieve the situation. A representative of the P.U.P. affiliate, the Christian Democratic Union, offered his Union's full support in a move to assist the working class, and invited the N.I.P. to be represented on the Union's Labor Committee to present a united front to relieve the labor situation.[xvii]
- The Party's Constitution and Standing Orders were adopted, as was its Program and Policy which covered constitutional, economic, social, labor and defense matters affecting Belize.

- The Party Leader officially unfurled and displayed the Party's flag[39] on August 1, 1958 at a dance in the Riverside Hall. It was a significant moment as the people stood at attention to the playing of "Sons of Honduras".

The matter of unemployment soon came up again when on August 12, 1958 Party Leader Fuller, in a letter to the Acting Governor, called his attention to the growing number of unemployed persons throughout Belize. The Acting Governor met a five-person N.I.P. delegation at Government House on August 20, in the presence of Government Members Albert Cattouse, Denbigh Jeffery and Enrique Depaz. At the end of the discussions Fuller felt hopeful that some jobs would be made available for the unemployed. By September 1958 the N.I.P. had opened its official headquarters at Tucker's building on Bishop Street in Belize City. The first branches of the Party also began to be formed in the district towns during 1958:

- The Stann Creek branch was inaugurated on September 21 under Alfred Ramirez as Chairman, Walter Slusher Deputy Chairman and Lorenzo Benguche as Secretary.
- The Corozal branch was established on September 28 with William Gegg as Chairman and Gerado Castenada, Secretary.
- On October 8 the Cayo branch had Hamid Musa as its Chairman and Percival Middleton as Secretary.

---

[39]The N.I.P. flag consisted of an oblique bar of white with bordering triangles of red with the letters NIP inscribed in the center.

- In Orange Walk on October 19 George Flowers was elected Chairman and Valentino Hopun as Secretary.
- The Punta Gorda branch was formed on October 27 with Bernard Avilez as Chairman and John Gentle, Secretary.
- Branches of the Party were also formed in the communities of Monkey River, Barranco, Burrel Boom, Santana and Maskall.

Agitating for constitutional advance, the Party saw the need for more elected members in the Executive Council as well as the implementation of a Ministerial system of government to give the people's representatives more power. The Party Leader, in a National Day address at Liberty Hall in 1958, therefore proposed that the P.U.P. and the N.I.P. set up a Joint Constitutional Reform Committee to present to the United Kingdom a demand for a new constitution.

City Council Election 1958

In preparation for the Belize City Council election in December 1958 the Party, at a membership meeting on October 16 in Liberty Hall, presented six candidates: Herbert Fuller, Jaime Staines, Claire Gill, Edward Flowers, Carl Rogers and Charles Lewis. The campaign platform centered on the alleged P.U.P. ties with Guatemala, culminating two days before the election with a "No Guatemala" demonstration having the participation of thousands of citizens.

In the midst of the election campaign it was found that two members of the N.I.P., Floss Casasola and James Meighan who had not been nominated to contest the City Council election, were charged with campaigning as independent candidates. Having broken their signed pledges to the Party by that action, the N.I.P. Executive Committee expelled them from the Party on November 5, 1958.

The Party gained representation on the Belize City Council when, on election-day December 15, 1958, Herbert Fuller, Jaime Staines, Claire Gill and Carl Rogers were elected. Although gaining only four seats to the P.U.P.'s five, and receiving 2,480 (49%) of votes cast, the Party was convinced that it had achieved two things: strengthened the organization it had built up and shown solidarity against the Guatemalan wish to incorporate Belize.

Constitution Committee

In January 1959 the N.I.P. set up a Constitution Committee headed by Herbert Fuller. Its task was to draft proposals for a new constitution; as well as to study ways for the improvement of the voting system in municipal elections. Shortly after, on February 26, a six-person delegation comprising Herbert Fuller, Jaime Staines, Philip Goldson, Denbigh Jeffery, Nicholas Pollard and Enrique Depaz met with the Governor to discuss constitutional advance for the upcoming general election. The Party Leader took the opportunity to request the Governor to invite a commissioner from Britain to discuss constitutional advance.

The Deputy Party Leader James Meighan, who had been expelled in 1958, was replaced by Jaime Staines at a meeting held on February 18, 1959. At the same meeting Edward Flowers was elected Party Chairman.

Party Policies

The N.I.P. from its inception operated under a system of strict policies, and to maintain that standard delegates representing branches from all over the country converged on Liberty Hall on February 27, 1959 for the opening of an Organization Planning Conference. The purpose of the Conference was for the Party to have better consolidation so that it would be a continuing force in local politics; that it operated efficiently yet democratically; that its members be politically educated; and that Party policy be developed from the informed opinion and decisions of all ranks of the Party and not from one individual.

Affiliation with the Western Independent Party

Benque Viejo was the last town to form a branch of the N.I.P. On April 12, 1959 a committee was elected naming Juan Gongora as Chairman and Javier Castellanos as Deputy Chairman. Incidentally a few days later, on April 29, a party calling itself the Western Independent Party was formed in Benque Viejo, and immediately sought affiliation with the N.I.P. Because the Western Independent Party was comprised of the same officers heading the N.I.P. branch it was easy to effect an affiliation. Juan Gongora became the Party Leader, and other members were: Javier Castellanos, Eduardo Guerra, Pastor Kotch, Aurelio Guerra, Benjamin Rosado, Medardo Bannos and Luis Gongora.

Visit of Sir Hilary Blood

In May, 1959 the Party, in a letter to the Secretary of State through the Governor, made a formal request to convene a conference in London to discuss all outstanding political, economic and security matters affecting Belize. It was further suggested that representatives of the three major political parties[40] attend the talks, and that the conference coincide with the Government delegation which was going to London for financial talks.

In preparation for the visit of Sir Hilary Blood, Constitutional Commissioner in September, the N.I.P., along with the Christian Democratic Party (C.D.P.),[41] in August drew up a set of proposals which it presented on September 3. Some of the more important proposals were:

- Establishment of the Ministerial system.
- A new constitution to confer internal self-government on Belize by 1960.
- Setting up a Legislature comprising a House of Representatives of 18 members, and a Senate of 11 members.
- Provision of a Cabinet presided over by a Prime Minister and nine other members.
- The Governor to retain control of Security, Justice, the Civil Service and Foreign Affairs.
- Belize City should in itself be a single electoral division.

---

[40]Apart from the P.U.P. and the N.I.P. existing in 1959 there was the Democratic Agricultural and Labour Party, which was formed in 1958, and was popularly known as the Christian Democratic Party.
[41]The Christian Democratic Party was established as the Democratic Agricultural and Labour Party in 1958.

First Annual Conference

The N.I.P. held its first Annual Conference on November 13, 1959 at Liberty Hall with Chairman Flowers acting as Conference Chairman. Officers elected were:

Herbert Fuller	Party Leader
Jaime Staines	Deputy Party Leader
Edward Flowers	Chairman
Charles Lewis	Deputy Chairman
Philip Goldson	Secretary
Lindsay Burns	Assistant Secretary
Magnus Vernon	National Organizer

The Conference approved the setting up of two committees. The first was the Political Policy Committee which drew up guidelines for political policy aimed at full internal self-government supported by the Blood Report as a practical step towards that goal. The second was the Economic Planning Committee which produced a plan for national prosperity and which was geared as the economic program and policy of the N.I.P. To ensure that the plan for national prosperity was put into effect the Conference approved the appointment of a "Shadow Ministry".

Town Board Elections 1959

Town Board elections were held in Stann Creek on December 28, 1959. Felix Martin and Harry Stanley won two seats for the N.I.P. by gaining 49.625% of the votes, while the P.U.P. got three seats with 50.375% of the votes cast.

Party Representation in London

Early in 1960 N.I.P. leaders joined with other political parties to form a delegation to discuss constitutional and economic matters in London. Herbert Fuller and Philip Goldson represented the N.I.P. at the conference which opened on February 1 and lasted for three weeks. The union of parties proved to be most successful as evidenced by the beneficial outcome:

- The Colonial Office was impressed by the unity and showed this by granting more assistance than if separate representations had been made,
- The Constitution Commissioner, Sir Hilary Blood himself, publicly expressed delight that a greater measure of constitutional advance than he had recommended had been granted to the delegation.
- The Guatemalan claim was denounced by the United Front.

Proposed Merger

In mid-February, 1960 a correspondent for the Daily Clarion suggested that the N.I.P. and the C.D.P. should merge, arguing that in so doing they had a better chance of winning the upcoming general election. For his part the Party Leader did not favor the idea and denied all rumors of a merger. In August, Claire Gill who was an active Party member and had been elected to the Belize City Council on a N.I.P. ticket, resigned from the Party. Describing herself as a 'Pollardite' she was opposed to the N.I.P.'s Executive Committee maintaining a policy of non-association with the C.D.P. of which Nicholas Pollard was a leader.

The N.I.P. began publishing a monthly magazine Newdeal on October 20, 1960. Selling for ten cents a copy it featured articles and news stories on national and Party matters.

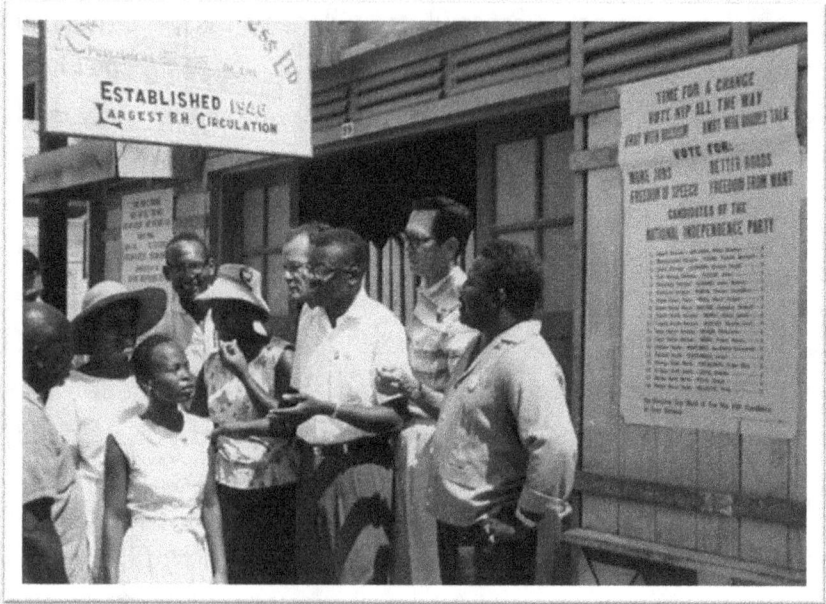

Figure 16 - Philip Goldson

General Election 1961

As the N.I.P. geared up for the general election of 1961 Herbert Fuller at a Courthouse Wharf meeting in January had to reiterate that, contrary to unfounded persistent rumors, the Party had no arrangements to merge, associate or form a united front with the C.D.P., the P.U.P. and any independent or splinter groups for the 1961 elections. At the second Annual Conference held at Liberty Hall in early February, following an

'Election Charge,' the following candidates contesting the election pledged loyalty to the Party's constitution, principles and policies:

Floss Casasola	Albert
Edward Flowers	Collet
Herbert Fuller	Fort George
Sabino Savery	Freetown
Erlean Casasola	Mesopotamia
Jaime Staines	Pickstock
Marcelo Casasola	Belize Rural North
Todd Brown	Belize Rural South
Ignacio Vega	Orange Walk South
Eloy Escalante	Orange Walk North
Victor Greenwood	Corozal South
Gualberto Martinez	Corozal North
Pedro Mena	Cayo South
Charles Westby	Toledo North
Francis Martinez	Toledo South
Paul Guerrero	Stann Creek Town
Harry Stanley	Stann Creek Rural

The Party suffered total defeat on election-day March 1, 1961 as the P.U.P. won all 18 elected seats in the Legislative Assembly. Of the total votes cast the N.I.P. received 5,107. Philip Goldson was named by the Governor as one of the five nominated members on the Legislative Assembly.

Philip Goldson as Party Leader

Herbert Fuller was away in Jamaica during April and May of 1961 undergoing major surgery. Still not well enough by September 1961 he had a message read at a Courthouse

Wharf meeting calling on all people who formed the opposition to the P.U.P. government to unite in one grand endeavor to defeat the common enemy. By year's end Fuller, due to ill-health, relinquished his post to Philip Goldson who was elected Party Leader. Fuller, who had earned the title Founder-Leader, passed away on March 11, 1962 at the age of 49.

The relocating of the Party's Headquarters to Liberty Hall in October prompted a *Belize Billboard* editorial of October 8, 1961 to comment that the move was intended "for the N.I.P. members and supporters to promote vigorous activities tending towards the firm establishment of a second strong political party for the country".

Early in 1962 Party Leader Goldson registered surprise over a statement that First Minister Price made to a Newsweek correspondent to the effect that Guatemala was friendly to Belize. It was Goldson's firm conviction that, if Guatemala had any real friendship for Belize, it would in good faith immediately discontinue its unfounded claim. The N.I.P.'s stand on the matter was clearly a desire for the people to live in harmony with their Guatemalan neighbors so that when Belize gained independence the people would still be in possession of the whole land "from the Hondo to the Sarstoon".[42] Goldson further asserted that before independence became a reality the leaders of Belize "must seek ironclad guarantees from friendly nations like Mexico,

---

[42]The Hondo and the Sarstoon are rivers which delineate the northern and southern borders of Belize respectively.

the United States, the West Indies, Great Britain, Canada and others that our country will be protected from aggression".

Party Demonstrations

To counter Guatemala's persistent claims to Belize as evidenced by the incursion of armed Guatemalans at Belize's southern border in January of 1962, and the insistence of the P.U.P. in displaying the Guatemalan colors publicly in Belize City, the N.I.P. sponsored a demonstration on March 3, 1962 to protest Guatemala's claim to Belize. Thousands of citizens marched through the streets and presented a memorial to the Governor asking for:

- The establishment of a Belize Battalion.
- The impending conference among the governments of Belize, Great Britain and Guatemala to be held in Belize.
- Majority and opposition parties, as well as Mexico, to be fully represented at the Conference.

Just over one month after the first demonstration, on April 11 the Citizens' Demonstration of Protest was held. Another memorial, this one protesting the composition of the Belize delegation to the Puerto Rico Conference, was handed to the Governor for transmission to the Secretary of State. The N.I.P.'s objection to Belize being represented by George Price, Albert Cattouse and Louis Sylvestre was that they were alleged to be Fifth Column agents of Guatemala.

In response to the N.I.P.'s first memorial of March 3, the Secretary of State responded saying that he did not consider

Belize a suitable place to hold the Puerto Rico talks, and furthermore saw no valid reason why the N.I.P. should be represented at the talks. Goldson, nevertheless, attended the conference on April 16, 1962 as a member of the press.

Institutional Strengthening

The Party sought to strengthen its organizational structure when on July 4, 1962 it formed the Albert Division Organization; and on July 11 the male section formed the 'Liberty Force' at a Liberty Hall meeting. Edward Flowers, Second Deputy Leader, was elected to be the National President of the latter organization and other officers included Lester Reyes, Leigh Richardson Sr. and Karl Mahler.

The Stann Creek Branch of the N.I.P. held its annual general meeting on August 12, 1962 and elected Albert Arzu as President, Sam Daniels Vice-President and Alfred Ramirez Chairman.

In Early September 1962 Jane Tweedy, a British public relations adviser, wrote a chapter in a publication titled "Imperial Postscript: the Smaller Territories" stating that there were three choices for Belize's future:

- Independence: The fundamental difficulty here was that Belize had neither the population nor the resources to stand alone, and therefore this was not a viable option.
- Federation: It was proposed that if Belize joined the "Little West Indian Federation" this would be the best situation because the country would still manage its

internal affairs while acceding to the political and economic principles of the Commonwealth.

- Self-government: This would become possible when Belize felt able to look the world in the face with greater confidence.

City Council Election 1962

Nine candidates to contest the Belize City Council election were selected at the Nominating Convention in the Thistle Hall on October 1, 1962. They were: Philip Goldson, Jaime Staines, Edward Flowers, Reginald Brooks, Helen Taylor, Rosita Williams, Leotine Gillette, Sabino Savery and Floss Casasola. In putting up nine candidates Party Leader Goldson felt that, under direct representation which had replaced proportional representation, the Party had a better chance of winning a majority.

The following month the N.I.P. published its "Manifesto for a Modern Belize" which contained pledges for the City Council to work as a team to re-plan, modernize and beautify Belize City. The Party's feeling at that time was that, because Belize was very close to achieving self-government and independence, the election would demonstrate whether there was a proper balance of political power and would have much more far-reaching significance than the municipal level. The Party further was of the opinion that if it won the election this would signify to observers in the United Kingdom and other countries that the two-party democratic system of government was assured for Belize; and in essence would show that the country could be entrusted with the responsibilities of self-government.

November 1962 saw Goldson protesting to the Minister of Education, J. Wilson Macmillan, in writing about the Government's use of the British Honduras Broadcasting Service to vilify the N.I.P. while denying it the right to reply through the same medium. The Minister's reply evasively stated that all candidates contesting the City Council election would be given free radio time as in the past, leading Goldson to conclude that the Minister made a "dishonest attempt to misunderstand the letter".

On election-day December 12, 1962 the N.I.P. lost the City Council election when all nine P.U.P. candidates were elected. The party felt, however, that 42.1% of the popular votes was a good percentage and that the two-party system was well on the way to becoming a reality. The Party closed the year with a resolve to continue the battle to establish democracy and to save the country from Guatemala.

Party Appointments

At a meeting chaired by Reginald Brooks at #54 George Street, Belize City, the "Independence" group of the Mesopotamia Division was formed during March 1963. The following month Party Leader Goldson declared open the First Plenary Session of the Annual Party Conference at the Riverside Hall. At the Second Plenary Session, held at Thistle Hall on April 27, officers were elected:

Philip Goldson	Party Leader
Jaime Staines	First Deputy Leader
Edward Flowers	Second Deputy Leader
Colville Young	Third Deputy Leader
Lindsay Burns	First Secretary
Sabino Savery	Deputy First Secretary

Appointments made by the National Executive Committee:

Helen Taylor	Financial Secretary
Reginald Brooks	Chief Organizer
Kenneth Mitchell	Transport & Equipment Officer

Leonie Vega and Aurora Rejon were elected President and Vice-President respectively of the Orange Walk Branch of the Women Pioneers on May 16, 1963.

Protestation and Picketing

The N.I.P. protested vigorously against the unequal party representation[xviii] at the upcoming self-government talks in London. The *Belize Billboard* of July 19, 1963 reported on the proposed protest actions:

> *"Historians will record the events which are scheduled to take place today as one of the great milestones in the history of British Honduras. Today, Wednesday July 10, marks the opening of the constitutional talks for self-government for British Honduras in London, as well as the protest demonstration to be staged by the N.I.P. against the one-party delegation representing British Honduras at that Conference, and also the 24-hour vigil and fast which the Leader of the N.I.P. began at 12 this morning, also in protest against the one-party delegation."*

The Party's delegation did not attend the Conference and Goldson said that he felt justified in taking such a position, explaining that when the Party said it was not going to London, and in fact did not go, it was more respected; and when it said it was prepared to make some sacrifice and showed it, it was also respected a little more.

In July 1963 the Guatemalan Government, under President Alfredo Enrique Peralta Azurdia, broke off diplomatic relations with Britain. Consequently Goldson, at a Courthouse Wharf meeting on July 30 called on the Consul-General of Guatemala to leave Belize within 24 hours. The next day Goldson and some supporters picketed the Guatemalan Consulate.

A booklet entitled "Political Facts about British Honduras, including Pattern of Betrayal to Guatemala" was published in early August 1963 by the N.I.P. Central Office and sold for 10 cents.

Town Board Elections 1963

Town Board elections for all towns were scheduled to be held before the end of 1963 and candidates were selected to contest the election. On election-day, December 27, the N.I.P. won in the towns of Orange Walk and Benque Viejo del Carmen.

Meeting with Nigel Fisher

The year 1964 opened with the visit of Nigel Fisher, Under-Secretary of State for the Colonies, with whom the N.I.P. held discussions at Government House on January 16. One week later the Party Leader declared at the weekly mass meeting at the Courthouse Wharf that the N.I.P. was the Party to lead Belize into independence, which was the reason the Party had been formed.

———————

Early in April German Ayuso resigned from the Orange Walk Town Board, and in a bye-election held on April 9 Eugene Flowers defeated the P.U.P. candidate Belizario Carballo.

———————

The Annual Party Conference was held on June 28 and one of the highlights of the second and final plenary session was the re-election of Philip Goldson as Party Leader. Other officers were:

Jaime Staines	First Deputy Leader
Colville Young	Second Deputy Leader
Edward Flowers	Third Deputy Leader

General Election 1965

Towards the end of 1964 candidates were chosen to represent the N.I.P. in the 1965 general election:

Philip Goldson	Albert
Colville Young	Mesopotamia
Edward Flowers	Collet
Helen Taylor	Fort George
Jaime Staines	Pickstock
Tharine Rudon	Freetown
Albert Arzu	Stann Creek Town
Augustus Buller	Stann Creek Rural

Edwin Morey	Toledo North
Charles Westby`	Toledo South
Teodocio Ochoa	Cayo North
Pedro Mena	Cayo South
Gualberto Martinez	Corozal North
Isidro Castaneda	Corozal South
Felipe Escalante	Orange Walk North
Erlindo Leiva	Orange Walk South
Elwyn Pitts	Belize Rural North
Philip Gillette	Belize Rural South

The N.I.P. won two seats, Philip Goldson and Edwin Morey, in the March 1, 1965 general election. Goldson polled 1,422 votes which was the highest number received by any candidate in the election.

Shadow Cabinet

In an unprecedented move at the end of March the Party Leader announced the formation of a Shadow Cabinet. Goldson reasoned that, now that the N.I.P. officially formed the elected opposition in the House of Representatives, the Party should not only provide a good and vigorous opposition but should also be ready to produce an alternate government any time it was called upon to do so. The functions of the Shadow Cabinet would be to advise and assist members of the opposition in the House and the Senate[43] to establish the principles and practices of a parliamentary opposition and to develop the nucleus of a future N.I.P. government. Although

---

[43]The Governor, on the advice of the Leader of the Opposition, had appointed Reginald Brooks and Simeon Hassock as Senators.

there were seven Government Ministers the Party Leader said that, for the time being, he was naming only six shadow ministers:

Philip Goldson	Finance, Planning, Information & Broadcasting
Edwin Morey	Local Government & Social Development
Dean Lindo	Natural Resources, Trade & Economic Development
Edward Flowers	Internal Affairs & Health
Colville Young	Education & Housing
Albert Arzu	Labor

Party Growth

The Annual Party Conference opened at Riverside Hall on June 25 with Philip Goldson as the keynote speaker. In his address he informed the gathering that the N.I.P. had grown 50 times as fast as the P.U.P. countrywide within the past four years and more than 100 times as fast in Belize City. He produced statistics to show that the P.U.P. had barely gained 300 new voters in the City between the 1961 and the 1965 general elections. The N.I.P., on the contrary, had gained more than 3,000 new voters in the City and he felt that it was only a matter of time before the Party became the Government. Goldson was unanimously re-elected Party Leader and other officers were:

Edward Flowers	First Deputy Leader
Colville Young	Second Deputy Leader
Leotine Gillett	Third Deputy Leader

Meeting with Anthony Greenwood

On October 12, 1965 a delegation of the N.I.P. met with Secretary of State for the Colonies Anthony Greenwood at Government House. The main points discussed were:

- Fair elections through honest registration and a fair voting system.
- The national symbols of Belize should be selected through a National Symbols Commission comprising of both parties. .
- Elections to be held before independence.
- Proper arrangements put in place for the security of the country.

City Council Election 1965

In preparation for the Belize City Council elections Party delegates within Belize City met at Riverside Hall on October 20 and selected nine persons: Edward Flowers, Howell Longsworth, Helen Taylor, Leotine Gillett, Colville Young, Rolando Perdomo, Claire Gill, Abel Rudon and Allan Anderson. On election-day, December 14, 1965 the N.I.P. received 45.738% of total votes cast but was unable to secure any of the nine seats.

The keynote speaker at the opening of the Eighth Annual Party Conference at Harley's Lot on March 31, 1966 was Simeon Hassock who spoke on the subject of independence. In officially declaring the Conference open at the Riverside Hall   the following night the Party Leader dwelled on three resolutions submitted by the National Executive Council:

- Reform of the electoral system.
- Proportional representation in all elections.
- Party policy on the question of independence.

The resolutions, after discussion by the delegates, were unanimously passed. At election time Philip Goldson was re-elected Party Leader, with other officers being:

Edward Flowers	First Deputy Leader
Leotine Gillett	Second Deputy Leader
Simeon Hassock	Third Deputy Leader

In a Town Board bye-election held in Stann Creek on July 14, 1966 N.I.P. candidate Albert Arzu defeated the P.U.P. candidate Carl Ramos.

The Toledo Branch of the Party held its annual convention at La Favorita Hall on September 30 and elected officers:

Francis Martinez	President
Benjamin Westby	First Vice-President
Erminio Norales	Second Vice-President
Pearl Apolonio	Secretary
Ivy Usher	Assistant Secretary
Charles Westby	Treasurer

Of the 49 candidates that contested the Town Board elections on December 28, 1966 the N.I.P. made some gains by winning 22 seats with representations in five towns and control of three.

First Planning Conference 1967

At the First Planning Conference of N.I.P. Mayors and municipal councilors held in Stann Creek Town on January 28, 1967 Albert Arzu called on all councilors countrywide to form a National Municipal League which was to be a united body to improve themselves as councilors and to create interest in improved methods of local government. A pro-tem Council of Management was comprised of:

Albert Arzu	President
Augustus Buller	Vice-President
Joseph Andrews	Secretary
Maurice Leslie	Treasurer

The Party's Ninth Annual Conference opened in St. Mary's Hall on April 7, 1967 and elected officers were:

Philip Goldson	Party Leader
Edward Flowers	First Deputy Leader
Dean Lindo	Second Deputy Leader
Colville Young	Third Deputy Leader

Meeting with Premier Price

The Party Leader met with Premier Price on August 14, 1967 to discuss national matters and to stress the opposition Party's demand for a referendum on the Anglo-Guatemalan mediation. The talks touched on other subjects like voter registration system, new general elections, national symbols, defense, History of Belize, Radio Belize, and economic conditions.

In August the Party Leader, while in New York, addressed the United Nations Special Committee on Decolonization requesting a speedy intervention to end the Guatemalan threat which was retarding the economic, political and social progress of Belize.

Political Calendar 1968

The N.I.P. began its 1968 political calendar by holding an "All-Belize" meeting at Liberty Hall on January 9. The Party Leader was the main speaker who, during the course of the meeting, introduced Rolando Perdomo and Teodocio Ochoa as new Shadow Ministers.

The first public meeting for the year was held on January 25 at Freedom Lane when Goldson addressed the gathering citing malpractices in the voting system and calling for election reforms.

Some Divisional Conferences were held early in 1968. The Stann Creek Division on February 11 supported a resolution by the Town Board seeking funds from Central Government for improvements in the Town. Elected as President of the Division was Mayor Albert Arzu. Two days later, in Belize City, the Fort George Division re-elected Allan Anderson as President. The Toledo North Division in March elected C. J. Avilez as President.

The first of two demonstrations during 1968 took place on February 23 with the people demanding that "Government be frank, honest and above board with the people of the country on vital issues, especially so on the matter of independence".

The Party's Tenth Annual Party Conference, held in Liberty Hall on March 22, re-elected Philip Goldson as Party Leader unopposed. Other officers elected were:

Edward Flowers	First Deputy Leader
Dean Lindo	Second Deputy Leader
Colville Young	Third Deputy Leader

The Webster Proposals

April 1968 saw the Government preparing to send a delegation to Washington to receive the proposals of Mediator Bethuel Webster for settlement of the Anglo-Guatemalan dispute over Belize. The N.I.P., although dissatisfied with the small proportion of their representation, after careful deliberation decided to accept the Government's invitation. Philip Goldson, Edwin Morey and Dean Lindo left Belize on April 23 and returned on April 28. After the Webster Proposals were distributed and broadcast countrywide they were totally rejected. This prompted the second demonstration for the year, which the *Belize Billboard* described as the people's reaction to the Webster Proposals:

> *"Sunday May 5, 1968 will be famous in history as the date on which the biggest demonstration ever to take place in Belize demanded the resignation of the Government of the People's United Party for its part in the plot to sell out British Honduras to Guatemala."*

The National Executive Committee of the N.I.P., in addition to demanding immediate resignation of the P.U.P. government, called for a general election to be supervised by the United Nations and the Commonwealth Secretariat. The Party

Leader's request for permission for radio broadcast time to air the N.I.P. views on the Mediator's Proposals was refused.

———————

In a bye-election on June 1, 1968 to fill a vacant seat in the Stann Creek Town Board caused by the death of N.I.P. Councilor Maurice Leslie the N.I.P. candidate, Luke Palacio, was defeated by P.U.P. candidate Carlos Nolberto.

City Council Election 1969

Coming to the end of 1968 the N.I.P. held a Nominating Convention in Liberty Hall on November 18 and selected nine candidates to contest the City Council election to be held the following year: Helen Taylor, Ulric Fuller, Henry Fairweather, Colville Young, Edward Anderson, Edward Flowers, Frank McNab, Reginald Brooks and Rolando Perdomo. Rounding off activities for the year the Party held a rally at Freedom Lane. Addressing the gathering the Party Leader said that it was in the interest of all citizens, P.U.P. and N.I.P., alike, to preserve the unity and strength of the Opposition to ensure that Belize could continue each year to enjoy the freedom and security which the Opposition's vigilance had so far preserved.

The new team to build the new Belize, as the N.I.P. called the nine candidates contesting the City Council election on April 30, 1969, was presented to the people in January. The City Council was dissolved on April 18 and on election-day the P.U.P. got 44,255 votes to defeat the N.I.P. which received 38,908 of the 83,163 votes cast.

Addressing a public meeting at Freedom Lane two days after the election, Goldson prophetically stated in part: "I have a mission and so I must go on to the end of the road. That mission is to help put down roots of democracy in our country, to protect the self-respect and the dignity of our people and keep this country secure for its people." He continued by saying that all that mattered was for him to complete that mission and he ended with the loquacious statement that the present leaders of Government, both in their personal and public conduct, tended to draw the people towards evil; and by the way they voted it appeared that the people liked it "so we can expect the condemnation of mankind and the vengeance of God to fall on our country".

Call for Defense Guarantee

The question of a British defense guarantee for Belize after independence was a constant topic in N.I.P. circles. Simeon Hassock, addressing an All-Belize meeting in Liberty Hall on June 8, 1969, felt that Britain was morally obliged to provide the country with some form of defense because, in as much as Britain had stood by Belize over the years, she had not taught it to defend itself.

Goldson's Leadership Opposed

Commenting on the Party's Eleventh Annual Delegates Conference which opened on June 27, 1969 at Bayvue Hall, a *Belize Billboard* editorial observed that it was the first Conference since the rejection of the Webster Proposals in 1968 and as such marked a turning point in the Party's mission. The editorial suggested that since the N.I.P. had convinced the country that the Proposals should be rejected, it could then pay more attention to the economic, social and political issues and problems of the people. When it came time for the Conference to elect officers Philip Goldson, although being openly opposed by Dean Lindo for leadership, was re-elected Party Leader with 110 votes to Lindo's 71. Other officers were:

Edward Flowers	First Deputy Leader
Ignacio Vega	Second Deputy Leader
Elfreda Reyes	Third Deputy Leader

In an effort to sustain mass support for the Party, Goldson, towards the end of July 1969, conducted a 9-day tour of the southern and western districts. He found "the Party everywhere strong, intact and growing". He even confidently commented to a reporter: "Our N.I.P. members and supporters in the districts are standing by their Party as we enter this second phase of the great struggle to save and build our country."

At every opportunity the Party Leader declared his gratitude for the people's dedication as exemplified at a Freedom Lane meeting on October 1, 1969. He assured the gathering that he had never lost faith in the people and asked that they continue to show the same faith in the N.I.P. which had led them "through obstacle after obstacle to save and preserve our country".

Meeting with Lord Shepherd

On October 3, 1969 Goldson led his followers in a demonstration which presented a petition to Lord Shepherd, visiting British Minister of State for Dependent Territories, calling for British military protection after independence. Goldson then led a N.I.P. delegation to meet with Lord Shepherd on October 6, and during the course of the interview Lord Shepherd commented: "Great Britain is not holding you back from independence, but at the same time she is not pushing you into it either. It is entirely up to the Government and people. They will get it when they ask for it." Significantly he evaded the question about a security guarantee for Belize.

General Election 1969

The N.I.P. had fought long and hard in opposition for almost a dozen years so that, when the House of Representatives was dissolved on November 7, 1969 to make way for a new general election, the N.I.P. expressed renewed confidence in winning. This was bolstered by Goldson's announcement on November 10: "The National Independence Party and the People's Development Movement[44] have agreed to contest the national elections as one body." Within the next few days the candidates for the N.I.P. -People's Development Movement (P. D. M.) were announced:

Philip Goldson	Albert
Dean Lindo	Fort George

---

[44]The People's Development Movement was formed in October 1969 under the leadership of Dean Lindo.

Edward Flowers	Collet
Colville Young	Mesopotamia
Charles Woods	Pickstock
Henry Fairweather	Freetown
Roy Canton	Belize Rural North
Allan Anderson	Belize Rural South
Gualberto Martinez, Jr.	Corozal North
Lucilo Teck	Corozal South
Felipe Escalante	Orange Walk South
Ignacio Vega	Orange Walk North
Joseph Andrews	Cayo North
Pedro Guerra Mena	Cayo South
Rodwell Leslie	Stann Creek Town
Albert Arzu	Stann Creek Rural
Edwin Morey	Toledo North
Cypriano Avilez	Toledo South

On election-day, December 5, 1969, Philip Goldson was the only N.I.P. -P. D. M. candidate elected while the P.U.P. won 17 seats. Of a total 29,823 registered voters the N.I.P. -P. D. M. received 40.68%, and the P.U.P. got 58.85% of the votes.

The final big political activity for 1969 was the Town Board elections held on December 29. The N.I.P. won all seven seats in Monkey River and held four seats in Orange Walk and three in San Ignacio. Overall the P.U.P. won a total of 35 seats to the N.I.P. 14.

Following several months of public silence the N.I.P. held a mass meeting on July 30, 1970 at which Party Leader Philip Goldson warned that Belize was headed for an economic crisis

173

brought about by the policies of the Government. He specifically pinpointed Belmopan,[45] the new capital city, which would greatly increase the cost of administration without increasing the wealth of the country or the revenues of Government.

Former Senator Reginald Brooks, who had been appointed to the National Assembly in 1965, resigned from the N.I.P. in 1970 "caused by distrust created after he was charged with disloyalty to the Party".

City Council Election 1971

In the Belize City Council election held on December 8, 1971 a coalition front of six N.I.P. candidates and three from the United Black Association for Development (U.B.A.D.)[46] was defeated when all nine seats were won by the P.U.P.

The Party contested Town Board elections on December 8, 1972 winning only in San Ignacio.

Amalgamation of Parties

With negligible success in both general and municipal elections since its inception in 1958, and with Party Leader Goldson leaving the country to pursue his legal education in the 1970s, the N.I.P. sought to strengthen its public image by

---

[45]Belmopan is located 50 miles inland from the former capital, Belize City. The government was moved to Belmopan in 1970 following the destruction of Belize City by hurricane Hattie in 1961.

[46]The United Black Association for Development was formed out of the United Black Culture Association and declared a political party in 1970.

amalgamating with the P. D. M. and the Liberal Party[47] to form the United Democratic Party in 1973.

The Democratic Agricultural and Labour Party – 1958 (Later called The Christian Democratic Party)

Just over one month after the formation of the N.I.P. Enrique Depaz,[48] at a small meeting on August 19, 1958 moved a resolution that a political party be formed "in view of the fact that to date there was still no effective opposition to George Price and the P.U.P. the coming into being of a third party was justifiable". His proposal that the name of the Party be the Democratic Agricultural and Labour Party (D.A.L.P.) was passed unanimously with Nicholas Pollard being elected provisional Party Leader. A Steering Committee comprised: Enrique Depaz, Hector Locke, Justo Pollard, Simon Young and Ernest Cain. Like most other parties formed in the 1950s the D.A.L.P.'s aim was chiefly to achieve self-government within the British Commonwealth, while pursuing the following goals:

- Cooperation with any and all individual political parties in any endeavor that was for the good of Belize.
- Formation of a coalition with any other minority group to destroy the treachery of the P.U.P.
- Promotion of a strong program for the social, economic and political development of the country.

---

[47]The Liberal Party was a new party formed in the early 1970s and headed by Manuel Esquivel.

[48]Enrique Depaz was a Member of the Legislative Assembly having been elected on a P.U.P. ticket in March 1957. He had resigned from the P.U.P. one year later.

- Educating the people on their rights, duties and wise conduct.
- Abstaining from entering the West Indies Federation or any political association with Guatemala or Central America.

Nicholas Pollard as Party Leader

The Party joined a 'No Guatemala' demonstration on December 13, 1958 organized by the N.I.P., when Party Leader Pollard also addressed the gathering. In unrelated developments Pollard, who for eight years had made repeated applications for his citizenship to be transferred from Mexican to British, was informed on December 16, 1958 that his naturalization as a British subject had been approved by Her Majesty's Government.

Early in January 1959 Pollard, in a letter to the *Belize Billboard*, expressed the view that the P.U.P. had been "put on the spot" because of a speech the Governor had made on December 29, 1958. The Governor had been speaking at the inaugural session of the Legislative Assembly calling for "overwhelming and uncompromising evidence" to refute Guatemalan propaganda claims that the people of Belize wanted to give up their British inheritance in favor of Guatemalan sovereignty. Although P.U.P. Leader, George Price, had reiterated his Party's objective of self-government and self-determination within or outside the British Commonwealth Pollard was still of the opinion that the P.U.P. would no doubt, with Guatemala's approval, pretend to oppose the Guatemalan claim.

Meeting with Sir Hilary Blood

The D.A.L.P., together with the N.I.P., on February 19, 1959 held a mass meeting at the Courthouse Wharf which opened a series of discussions on a new constitution. One week later a six-man delegation, comprising four from the N.I.P. and two from the D.A.L.P., met with the Governor to discuss constitutional advance for 1960. When Constitution Commissioner Sir Hilary Blood arrived in Belize later in the year the D.A.L.P., at that time popularity called the Christian Democratic Party (C.D.P.),[xix] sent a delegation to hold discussions with him. The delegation was comprised of Party Leader Nicholas Pollard, Deputy Leader Enrique Depaz, Secretary Robert Taylor, along with Richmond Fitzgibbons and Rupert Cain.

Only into the second year of its existence observers felt that the C.D.P. was too weak on its own. A correspondent, writing in the Daily Clarion of February 24, 1960, was "obliged to denounce what he considers the errors of the N.I.P. leadership, but the N.I.P. and the C.D.P. still remain his favorite political parties. The N.I.P. and the C.D.P. must win the first General Election under the coming new constitution. And one of the first steps toward that end should be a merger of the two parties."

Denbigh Jeffery as Party Leader

The merger of the N.I.P. and the C.D.P. was not long in coming, but before that apparently the C.D.P. wanted to independently test its strength against the P.U.P. Its only concession was made on October 12, 1960 when Pollard announced that Denbigh Jeffery[49] had assumed leadership of the C.D.P. The plan to reorganize had apparently taken place the previous night at a joint meeting of the N.I.P. Executive and the Citizens Committee when Pollard stepped down as Leader, supported Jeffery as the new Leader and Jeffery's nomination was unanimously accepted. Election of officers resulted in:

Nicholas Pollard	Deputy Leader
Lionel Francis	Chairman
Mervyn Hulse	Secretary
Ernest Cain	Assistant Secretary
Claire Gill	Treasurer
Robert Taylor	National Organizer

Other members of the Executive Council were: Enrique Depaz, Hubert Usher, Rupert Cain and Tasman Hinds.

Jeffery made it known immediately that his primary objective was to defeat the P.U.P. At the first major campaign meeting at the Courthouse Wharf on October 14, 1960 for the upcoming election, which was also the first public meeting of the reorganized Party, he called on the N.I.P. to join forces with the C.D.P. to "crush this wicked element that is in our midst".

General Election 1961

Early in 1961 the candidates contesting the general election were announced:

---

[49]Denbigh Jeffery had been expelled from the P.U.P. in 1957, and after serving on the N.I.P. Executive Committee he resigned to become a member of the C.D.P. in 1960.

Denbigh Jeffery	Fort George
Nicholas Pollard	Albert
Clare Gill	Pickstock
Ernest Cain	Freetown
Mervyn Hulse	Collet
Edward Usher	Mesopotamia
Eduardo Espat	Cayo South
Manuel Figuerroa	Cayo North
Tomas Salam	Toledo North
A. Woodye	Toledo South
Arthur Wade	Belize Rural North

On election-day, March 1, 1961, the C.D.P. received 11.4% of votes cast and failed to secure any seats as the P.U.P. won a sweeping victory.

The C.D.P. Disbanded

Words of exhortation for the C.D.P. to continue its fight and grow stronger came from several quarters. One writer in a May 1961 issue of the Daily Clarion stated in part:

> *"The C.D.P. is the youngest of our three political parties and the poorest of them all; but I sincerely feel that it is destined to play a great part in the efforts of the righteous to make this land a better and happier place in which to live."*

The article ended by asking the leaders of the C.D.P. to ensure that they do not weaken before their great opportunity came, for it was bound to come.

With all that, the C.D.P. after a brief life of three years was disbanded in 1961 and became amalgamated with the N.I.P.

The Peoples' Independent Party – 1968

The Partido Independente del Pueblo (Peoples' Independent Party) was formed in the Corozal District on February 4, 1968. The Party's aim was to give Belize "the leadership necessary in its objectives of individual and collective liberty and its search for the welfare of the individual on the communal as well as national level".

Officers elected at the initial meeting were:

Lucilo Teck	Chairman
Romaldo Herrera	Treasurer
Tobias Mendez	Secretary
Damiano Mendez	Committee Member
Claudio Teck	Committee Member
Pedro Gonzalez	Committee Member

The officials of the Party promised never to depart from the democratic path nor violate the sacred rights of the individual; and pledged to accept the voice of the majority as well as to defend the rights of the minority. A national appeal was made for support of the Party which belonged to everyone, anticipating that it would provide the machinery necessary for the urgent advancement of the goals of liberty and national welfare.

The United Black Association for Development – 1968

Although not officially declared a political party until July 15, 1970 the United Black Association for Development (U.B.A.D.) actually was born at a lecture on Black History given by Evan

Hyde in September 1968 at the then Bliss Institute. Formerly titled the United Black Culture Association U. B. A. D, on February 9, 1969, adopted a constitution and elected Lionel Clark as President and Evan Hyde as Secretary. Apart from meeting on Wednesday nights to discuss tactics geared towards the development of Belize, the movement which described itself as cultural and educational gained a following by holding public meetings in Belize City and the district towns.

The social efforts of U.B.A.D. in the early days included a breakfast program for needy children and a bakery. Unfortunately, the latter closed down for lack of funding while the breakfast program suffered a similar fate when its chief transport person, Michael Allen, was deported to the U. S. A.

Figure 17 - Evan X Hyde

181

Peoples Action Committee

During 1969 the Peoples Action Committee (P.A.C.) was formed by Assad Shoman and Said Musa. Having similar views with U.B.A.D., its aim was "the changing of a corrupt and oppressive system to a system which ensures freedom, justice and equality for all". While U.B.A.D. emphasized the cultural aspects of the struggle, P.A.C. accented the political.

Revolitical Action Movement

In October 1969 U.B.A.D. and P.A.C. joined to form the Revolitical Action Movement (R.A.M.) and elected its officers:

Evan Hyde	President
Assad Shoman	Vice-President
Ismael Shabazz	Treasurer
Albert Faber	Chairman

Other executive members were: Calvin Avilez, William Stewart and Charles Eagan.

Seditious Conspiracy

The year 1970 was significant for two events. Firstly, R.A.M. was dissolved in January over policy disputes leaving U.B.A.D. to resume its solitary existence. Secondly, Evan Hyde and Ismael Shabazz were charged with seditious conspiracy on March 5. The allegation was that in February an article published in the Amandala,[50] entitled "Games Old People Play", inferred that the administration of justice was a farce

---

[50]The *Amandala* is a newspaper established since August 13, 1969, as the main mouthpiece of U.B.A.D.

and that the Chief Justice and counsels who participated in it were involved in a childish game of amusement. The Supreme Court case ended on July 7 with the acquittal of both men.

Demonstration

U.B.A.D. demonstrators marched through the streets of Belize City on July 13, 1970 making demands for:

- Eighteen-year old persons to be eligible to vote in elections.
- Radio time to be granted impartially to political parties.
- The creation of more jobs.
- The availability of more lands.
- African history to be taught in schools.

U.B.A.D. A Political Party

On July 15, 1970 U. B. A. D, which had gradually been moving into the political arena, officially declared itself a political party at a meeting in Liberty Hall. On August 12 officers were elected to the Executive:

Evan X Hyde	President
Galento X Neal	Vice-President
Charles X Stamp	Chairman
Lillette Barkley	Secretary-General
Ismael Omar Shabazz	Treasurer-General
Wilton Meighan	Officer
Raiford Wade	Officer
Michael Stephen	Officer
Clifford Leslie	Officer
Albert Betson	Officer

In November 1970 Evan X Hyde resigned as President, and Galento X. Neal was elected President. This was short-lived as the Annual General Meeting, held on February 28, 1971, saw the following elected to office:

Evan X Hyde	President
Galento X Neal	Vice-President
Rufus X	Chairman
Wilton Meighan	Secretary-General
Ismael Omar Shabazz	Treasurer-General
Wilfred Nicholas	Officer
Jack Jordan	Officer
Clifford Leslie	Officer

City Council Election 1971

The City Council election was coming up in December 1971 and in April the U.B.A.D. and the N.I.P. set up a joint working committee to discuss, among other issues, opposition radio time and the 18-year old vote. To emphasize the importance of those subjects, on June 25, the U.B.A.D. Party marched peacefully through the streets of Belize City demanding that the subjects be addressed immediately.

On election-day, December 8, 1971, the N.I.P.-U.B.A.D. nine coalition candidates comprising Evan X Hyde, Ismael Shabazz, Clifford Leslie, Rita Berry, Benjie Belisle, Hubert Gardiner, Thomas Abraham, Edney Bennett and M. E. Burgess were all defeated by the P.U.P.

Guatemalan Consulate Stoned

During the early months of 1972 the Party reiterated its principles, along with its stand in Belizean society, through public meetings held in Belize City and San Ignacio. At that point of its existence observers described U.B.A.D. as an organization which seemed very loose and undefined from the outside, but was in effect very tight, cohesive and disciplined internally. In connection with Pan African Liberation Week the Party sponsored a demonstration in Belize City on June 1, 1972 which ended in disarray. Demonstrators stoned the Guatemalan Consulate building while attacking various government and private offices along Albert and Regent Streets; and among those arrested by the Police was Norman Fairweather the publisher of the Amandala.

Internal Strife

In 1973, U.B.A.D., which touted itself as the "Party for Freedom, Justice and Equality," experienced some internal strife. In the first instance, with the formation of the United Democratic Party (U.D.P.) in September 1973, some of U.B.A.D.'s executive members left to join the U.D.P. Secondly, because it preferred not to become a part of the Unity Congress,[51] it was accused of leaning towards the P.U.P. In a November issue of the Amandala an explanation was given:

> *"What has been happening over the past few months is that* the Premier has adopted the foreign policy of the U.B.A.D.

---

[51]The Unity Congress was formed in 1973, consisting of the N.I.P., the People's Development Movement and the Liberal Party, to present a united force to contest the upcoming general elections.

*Party and has indicated he is willing to consider the
domestic policies of the U.B.A.D. in new light. So why should
we attack him when he does something we have
advocated?"*

General Election 1974

Early in 1974 the Party announced that President Evan X Hyde
would be a candidate in the upcoming general election and
would be contesting the Collet Division. The Party's platform
was:

- Voting rights for 18 year old Belizeans.
- Free radio and television.
- Proportional representation.
- Arming of the people.
- Land ownership for Belizeans.
- Workers and farmers empowered.
- Teaching of African and Mayan history.
- Independence for Belize.

The general election was held on October 30, 1974 and Evan
X Hyde lost[xx] in the Collet Division to Vernon Courtenay of the
P.U.P. Overall the P.U.P. won 12 of the 18 seats, while the
U.D.P. gained the other 6.

In a post-election statement the U.B.A.D. Party felt that its
principles and doctrines had served to affect both the P.U.P.
and the U.D.P.:

> *"A former U.B.A.D. member Assad Shoman is now Attorney
> General and Minister of Economic Planning. U.B.A.D.
> sympathizers like Philip Goldson and Paul Guerrero are now
> elected representatives of the people. Two other
> sympathizers, Said Musa and Theo Ochoa, are Senators.*

U.B.A.D. Disbanded

The U.B.A.D. Party phased itself out following the 1974 general elections, and officially had its 'swan song' in an *Amandala* November 8, 1974 article by Evan X Hyde entitled "A Farewell to Arms". Another postscript evolved in a reply Hyde made to a letter from the Leader of the Opposition, Dean Lindo, on the matter of the Guatemalan claim to Belize:

> *"I reply to you as the last President of U. B. A. D originally a cultural organization, then a political party and since November 1, 1974 unofficially and for all intents and purposes, disbanded. All that is left of U.B.A.D. is a feeling of spirit and the Amandala newspaper which has been attempting to give independent, impartial political reports."*

The U.B.A.D. legacy eventually extended itself into KREM Radio and KREM Television and can be said to have returned in 1994 as the U.B.A.D. Educational Foundation with Evan X Hyde as Chairman.

The People's Development Movement – 1969

Joining the National Independence Party (N.I.P.), which since 1958 was the bulwark of the people's opposition to the P.U.P., was the People's Development Movement (P. D. M.). This political party was formed in October 1969 with Dean Lindo[52] as Party Leader along with other officers:

Colville Young	Deputy Leader
Hugh Weir	Treasurer
Carlos Castillo	Secretary

---

[52]Dean Lindo, a lawyer, at that time had been in politics for over five years as a member and Deputy Leader of the N.I.P., but resigned after having failed to influence the policies and strategy of that Party.

187

Lawrence Young   Chairman of the National
                                 Council

The basic principles of the P. D. M. were described as "liberal in its economic and development policies and pragmatic in its approach to national problems". The Party formed a coalition with the N.I.P. and contested its first general election on December 5, 1969, which resulted in Philip Goldson of the N.I.P. securing a single seat to the P.U.P.'s 17.

Dean Lindo as Party Leader

The P. D. M. languished until it held its first public meeting on January 31, 1973 when Dean Lindo stated that his Party was prepared "to sit down and meet with any opposition group in an attempt to have opposition unity".

During March the Party issued a token objection to the change of the country's name from British Honduras to Belize on the grounds that "the Premier's Government is now seeking to put into effect Article 1 of Webster's 17 proposals which, in 1968, was rejected by the people". The P. D. M. felt that any change in the name of the country was a matter for the people which should be decided in a plebiscite including the 18 year olds.

Amalgamation

The hoped-for unity proposed in January 1973 after months of serious political discussion, came to fruition in August 1973 with the P. D. M., the N.I.P. and the new Liberal Party led by Manuel Esquivel agreeing to present a united force to contest the upcoming general election. By executive decision each party appointed three delegates to act on behalf of their respective parties at a proposed Unity Congress. On September 27, 1973 the Unity Congress issued a statement that it had formed itself into one political party called the United Democratic Party.

SECTION THREE
THE RISE OF THE UNITED DEMOCRATIC PARTY

The United Democratic Party – 1973

The United Democratic Party (U.D.P.) was formed on September 27, 1973 out of the National Independence Party (N.I.P.), the People's Development Movement (P. D. M.) and the Liberal Party as a display of unity among opposition parties. The Party held its first political meeting on January 16, 1974 at Harlem Square on Glynn Street in Belize City at which the keynote speech was given by Kenneth Tillett. On July 17 a Central Party Office was opened at 56 Albert Street.

General Election 1974

Contesting its first general election held on October 30, 1974 the U.D.P. won six seats to the P.U.P. 12. Although not a victory the U.D.P. viewed the outcome as a spell that had been broken, evidenced by:

- It was the first time in six terms going back more than 20 years that opposition parties were able to gain more than two seats in the 18-man House of Representatives.
- Three of the seats won by the P.U.P. – Collet, Pickstock and Corozal Town – represented a majority of only 17 votes.

The overall count showed that the P.U.P. polled 12,269 votes (52.66%) to 11,029 (47.34%) polled by opposition and independent candidates. Kenneth Tillett and Theodocio Ochoa were appointed as U.D.P. Senators.

Party Leader Dean Lindo

The U.D.P. had been functioning without a leader until November 1, 1974 when a release from headquarters announced that Dean Lindo had been appointed Party Leader, and Joseph Andrews Deputy Leader.

Figure 18 - Dean Lindo

City Council Election 1974

City Council election was scheduled to be held on December 11, 1974 and a convention at Birds Isle on November 25 selected nine candidates: Philip Goldson, Kenneth Tillett, Harry Lawrence, Paul Rodriguez, Curl Thompson, Collet Gill, Angus Vernon, Manuel Esquivel and Eric Neal. The results of the election showed the U.D.P. winning a majority of six seats[53] of the nine over the P.U.P. which had held all nine seats in the previous City Council. At a meeting of the new Council on December 18 Paul Rodriguez was elected Mayor and Curl Thompson as Deputy Mayor.

First Viable Opposition in the House

With a viable opposition in the House of Representatives the U.D.P., and with Party Leader Dean Lindo as Leader of the Opposition, the Party was well represented at foreign conferences. On June 7, 1975 Lindo travelled to London for a series of meetings with members of Parliament and the Secretary of State. The meetings were intended to gain first-hand information regarding the attitude of the British government towards independence for Belize.

Joint Opposition to Guatemalan Claim

The other important subject addressed by the U.D.P. was Guatemala's claim to Belize. Following a sitting of the House of Representatives on October 3, 1975 government announced that: "Following months of closed doors negotiations between the Government and opposition delegates the parties have finally agreed to join forces in making another appeal to the United Nations on the Guatemalan claim over Belize." The Opposition, which had always held the view that the Guatemalan claim to Belize was a serious one, welcomed the opportunity to reaffirm that stand and appointed Senator Theodocio Ochoa as the Opposition delegate to the United Nations.

---

[53]Unsuccessful candidates were Collet Gill, Angus Vernon and Eric Neal.

_____

Town Board elections were held on December 22, 1975 and the majority of seats were won by the P.U.P. For its part the U.D.P. won all seats in Punta Gorda, one in Stann Creek, one in San Ignacio and their allies, the Corozal United Front[xxi] won all seats in Corozal.

_____

In early 1976 Paul Rodriguez and Curl Thompson were re-elected Mayor and Deputy Mayor respectively by the Belize City Council.

Defection

Vicente Choco, who had been the U.D.P. elected representative for the Toledo North Division in the 1974 general election, defected to the P.U.P. in February 1976.

_____

At its first National Convention on April 4, 1976 the U.D.P. elected officers:

Manuel Esquivel	Chairman
Harry Lawrence	Vice-Chairman
Kenneth Tillett	Secretary General
Margaret Guerrero	Deputy Secretary General
Lionel Tillett	Director of Organization

Third Term Mayor

For a third term in succession the Belize City Council, in 1977, elected Paul Rodriguez and Curl Thompson as Mayor and Deputy Mayor respectively. The Party, at a meeting held on

March 7, 1977, inaugurated the U.D.P. Roll of Honor when some 90 persons were enrolled.

Demonstration for Referendum

The U.D.P. took a more cautious and guarded approach to the eventual attaining of independence than the P.U.P. Taking into account the several constraints, and wanting a more principled structure to achieve complete self-determination, the Party held a demonstration on July 10, 1977 to emphasize its call for a referendum before Belize reached independence status. Following a rally at the Courthouse Plaza Party Leader Dean Lindo led several hundred supporters in a spontaneous protest march along the Foreshore where they were confronted by armed soldiers of the paramilitary unit. Although violence was averted, because the police agreed for the demonstrators to detour through South Street back to the Foreshore, the incident was given prime broadcast time on the B. B. C.

City Council Election 1977

A Belize City Council election was held on December 7, 1977 and the U.D.P. candidates took all nine seats: Paul Rodriguez, Philip Goldson, Manuel Esquivel, Kenneth Tillett, Harry Lawrence, Lionel Tillett, Curl Thompson, Eudora Pitts and Jacqueline DeShield. At the inaugural meeting of the City Council Paul Rodriguez was elected as Mayor and Curl Thompson as Deputy Mayor.

Declaration on Independence

Moving confidently forward into 1978 the U.D.P. made a declaration on February 8 for a deferment of independence: "The independence of Belize should be deferred for a period of not less than ten years, and that the National Assembly should immediately adopt a resolution for a ten year moratorium." During February also the Party gained more support when the ruling party in the Corozal Town Board, the Corozal United Party, converted itself into the Corozal United Democratic Party and became one of the self-governing divisions of the U.D.P.

Goldson's House Suspension

The six U.D.P. members in the House of Representatives had an uphill battle in opposing the P.U.P. government and during one confrontation in the House on March 3, 1978 Philip Goldson was challenged by the Speaker on his right to speak. Goldson, in an attempt to assert his right, was suspended from the House for an indefinite period. Although this drastic action was branded by the U.D.P. as wrong and unjustifiable Goldson was not reinstated until July 7, 1978 in absentia.

New Party Officers

At the second biennial conference held on May 21, 1978 officers elected were:

Manuel Esquivel	Chairman
Theodore Aranda	First Deputy Chairman
Nestor Vasquez	Second Deputy Chairman

Israel Alpuche	Third Deputy Chairman
Lionel Tillett	Executive Secretary
Faith Stuart	Assistant Secretary
Collet Gill	Financial Secretary General
Philip Goldson	Director of Organization

Figure 19 - Manuel Esquivel

Town Board Elections 1978

Town Board elections were held on December 20, 1978 and the U.D.P. won 30 of the 49 seats contested in the seven towns. The U.D.P. viewed that victory as being the continued march of the electorate, as well the country, towards the ultimate goal: The New Direction.

196

Early in 1979 the selection of Mayors and Deputy Mayors for the five towns controlled by the U.D.P. resulted in:

Dangriga	Alonzo Ogaldez
	Margaret Guerrero
San Ignacio	Joseph Andrews
	Rene Montero
Corozal	Israel Alpuche
	Maria de Carmen Reyes
Punta Gorda	C. J. Avilez
	Eugene Martinez
Monkey River	Melvin Coleman
	Pearl Duncan

In Belize City Paul Rodriguez and Curl Thompson were re-appointed Mayor and Deputy Mayor for a further one year term.

General Election 1979

A general election was held on November 21, 1979 resulting in the P.U.P. winning 13 seats to the U.D.P. five: Theodore Aranda, Philip Goldson, Curl Thompson, Charles Wagner and Basilio Ah.[54] Those election results prompted great discontent among U.D.P. followers countrywide with claims that the election was stolen by the ruling P.U.P. by means of "rigged ballots printed by a friendly communist government". Hundreds of high school students attended a mass rally at the Pound Yard Bridge on November 30 and the following days saw the staging of large demonstrations.

---

[54]Party Leader Dean Lindo was defeated in his constituency.

Theodore Aranda as Party Leader

The representative for Dangriga, Dr. Theodore Aranda, was selected by the Party's Parliamentary Committee to be the Party Leader and was subsequently appointed Leader of the Opposition in the House of Representatives by the Governor. Philip Goldson became Deputy Leader and Curl Thompson Party Whip. Two appointments to the Senate, Manuel Esquivel and Elodio Aragon, were made by the Governor.

Tenaciously maintaining its earlier charge of election fraud, during the inaugural session of the House of Representatives, the elected members of the Party and the two Senators walked out as a group as the Governor was about to deliver his traditional speech. In a comment before exiting Aranda declared: "Mr. Speaker, with due respect to Her Majesty the Queen, we the Opposition cannot stay here today when those of the majority party have been fraudulently elected."

Kenneth Tillett, who had contested the Collet Division in the 1979 election, in a letter to the Secretary of the U.D.P. dated April 14, 1980 stated that he was withdrawing from active politics and he left the country shortly after. The Party continued the struggle in representing the people in any way it could, and August 3, 1980 saw a delegation comprising Theodore Aranda, Philip Goldson and Manuel Esquivel arriving in London for talks with officials of the Foreign and Commonwealth Office over the future of Belize.

City Council Election 1980

In the Belize City Council election held on December 17, 1980 about 66% of the 18,000 registered voters gave the P.U.P. the victory by winning all nine seats. The U.D.P. candidates were: Leroy Panting, Jacqueline DeShield, Manuel Esquivel, Curl Thompson, Philip Goldson, Eudora Pitts, Gustavo Bautista, Derek Aikman and Samuel Rhaburn.

National Symbols Commission

With the advent of Belize's independence some time in 1981 the Central Committee of the U.D.P. early in the year saw it fitting to adopt a proposed National Flag, while calling for a National Symbols Commission to consider the national symbols.

Heads of Agreement

A prominent feature of 1981 was the Heads of Agreement document which sought to offer a solution to the Guatemalan claim to Belize. Signed on March 11, 1981 in London the agreement, instead of being a base for negotiations between Great Britain, Belize and Guatemala, was rejected by the people and created countrywide protests. One of the more unpopular clauses in the agreement was summed up in a radio address by the Premier on March 16:

> *"To meet Guatemala's need for the sea access to the Caribbean Sea from the Gulf of Honduras and the Bay of Amatique Guatemala shall be assured of a sea passage with rights over the sea bed of such passage. This will be achieved by Belize limiting its territorial sea in our southern waters to the three-mile limit which we presently claim and enjoy. We will not give up any sea that we now own."*

On March 17 clashes occurred between citizens and the Police resulting in damage to properties, looting and several arrests. A state of emergency was declared by the Governor on April 2 and it was in this situation that Belize would become independent on September 21, 1981.

At constitutional talks regarding independence which started in London on April 6, 1981, the U.D.P. representatives, Dr. Theodore Aranda, Philip Goldson and Manuel Esquivel, boycotted the conference on the grounds of:

- A rapidly deteriorating situation in Belize due to the state of emergency and a nationwide strike of civil servants and teachers.
- The refusal of Minister of State Nicholas Ridley to postpone the conference long enough to enable him to come to Belize for on-the-spot consultations and observations.
- The Government feeding the news media half-truths and lies indicating a complete lack of good faith on their part in dealings with the Opposition.
- The non-materializing of commitments by the British Government of assurances since 1978 that the Opposition would participate in all Anglo-Guatemalan negotiations.

Independence Conditions

The U.D.P. had always been fully committed to the principle of independence for Belize but felt that before that was achieved there should be some conditions met. Those were categorically stated in mid-April of 1981:

- Find a just and peaceful solution to the Anglo-Guatemalan dispute.
- If (a) was not possible then the people be given the opportunity the express in a referendum whether they wished to go into independence without a solution to the dispute.
- Reform the Elections and Boundaries Commission and Radio Belize to allow political parties equal participation in those two public bodies.
- Britain to take the necessary steps to ensure Belize's future security.
- Britain to prepare Belize to enable it to participate meaningfully in its defense by land, sea and air.

After the March and April riots subsided, a delegation comprising of Carl Rogers, Vernon Courtenay and Assad Shoman of the P.U.P. attended negotiations on the Heads of Agreement on May 20, 1981 in New York. The U.D.P. further consolidated its rejection of the Heads of Agreement by declining an invitation from the Belize government to join the delegation, stating: "The Party believes that it cannot join in negotiations which are preconditioned to produce results so detrimental to the vital interests of Belize and so contrary to the expressed wishes of the Belizean people." That first round of negotiations had no results and two months later, at the invitation of Nicholas Ridley, Dr. Theodore Aranda and Manuel Esquivel left Belize to meet with Ridley. The delegation was able to extract a promise from him that he would urge the Premier to meet with the U.D.P. to try to resolve the many serious problems causing disunity in Belize, especially the issues connected with progress towards independence.

Independence

At midnight on September 21, 1981 the Union Jack was lowered for the last time and the new Belizean flag hoisted in its place.

> *"And so it was that on the 21st September 1981 Belize became an independent nation without rancor, without violence and with a fund of goodwill which should stand her in good stead for the future."*

During 1981 there were other events that had an effect on the U.D.P.

- On June 30 the former P.U.P. Minister of Trade and Industry, Santiago Perdomo, formally joined the U.D.P.
- In Town Board elections held on December 16 the U.D.P. gained control of three of the six main towns: Benque Viejo, San Ignacio and Dangriga.
- On December 29 the death of Joseph Andrews, age 37, occurred in Los Angeles. He had served as U.D.P. area representative for the Cayo North constituency in the House of Representatives from 1974 to 1979.

SECTION FOUR
SMALL PARTIES SINCE 1974

Following the formation of the U.D.P. in 1973, several small parties came on the political scene:

The Corozal United Front – 1974

The Corozal United Front (C.U.F.) was formed in 1974 under the leadership of Israel Alpuche. It was active only in Corozal and eventually became an affiliate of the U.D.P.

The Corozal United Party – 1978

Formed in 1978 the Corozal United Party (C.U.P.) converted itself into the Corozal United Democratic Party and became one of the self-governing divisions of the U.D.P.

The Toledo Progressive Party – 1979

The Toledo Progressive Party (T.P.P.) was formed by Alejandro Vernon in 1979 and was active only in Punta Gorda. It is now defunct.

The Christian Democratic Party – 1982

Active only in Dangriga, the Christian Democratic Party was formed by Dr. Theodore Aranda after he resigned from the U.D.P. in 1982. It is now defunct.

The Belize Popular Party – 1988

The Belize Popular Party (B.P.P.) was formed in 1988 by two members of the P.U.P.'s right wing, Fred Hunter and Louis Sylvestre, who had resigned, charging that the party had become too leftist in orientation. The B.P.P. was active in San Pedro, Ambergris Caye, during the 1988 town board elections and in the 1989 general election, but neither of its candidates won. The party is now defunct.

The San Pedro United Movement – 1989

Formed in the 1980s by Gilberto Gomez the San Pedro United Party (S.P.U.M.) is active only in San Pedro, Ambergris Caye. It contested municipal elections for the P.U.P.

SECTION FIVE
THIRD PARTY HOPEFULS

The National Alliance for Belizean Rights – 1991

The National Alliance for Belizean Rights (N.A.B.R.) came out of an organization called the Patriotic Alliance for Territorial Integrity which was formed on December 1, 1991. The Patriotic Alliance for Territorial Integrity was intended basically to oppose the passage of the Maritime Areas Bill, a proposed law which had been tabled in the House of Representatives by the P.U.P. government.

As a preface on August 14, 1991 the Guatemalan Government, under President Jorge Antonio Serrano Elias, stated that it was finally recognizing the right of the Belizean people to self-determination and would seek to have a definitive settlement of the territorial dispute. Two days later the government of Belize, after consulting the Opposition U.D.P., introduced a bill in the House of Representatives for a law to extend Belize's territorial seas to 12 miles[55] and provide for a 200-mile exclusive economic zone. This gesture was supposedly intended to be "a sign of good faith on the part of Belize to pursue negotiations with the Republic of Guatemala in search of a settlement of the outstanding dispute".

---

[55]In the south this would be limited to three miles.

Resignations over Maritime Areas Bill

Philip Goldson, elected U.D.P. representative for the Albert Division along with Derek Aikman, Hubert Elrington and Melvin Hulse senior, in protest of the passage of the law resigned from the U.D.P. and formed the Patriotic Alliance for Territorial Integrity. In an open letter to 'Patriotic Belizeans' they called on the people to reject the Maritime Areas Bill because "Our stand is that no Belizean land, sea or rights are up for negotiations". The fact that Belize should "offer territorial sea to Guatemala as reward and compensation for recognition of Belize's inherent right to independence cannot, and will not, be accepted by patriotic Belizeans". The letter reiterated that Belize should not further compensate Guatemala by giving away rights which belong to future generations; and concluded by inviting all to join the Patriotic Alliance for Territorial Integrity.

Patriotic Alliance for Territorial Integrity Goals

The Alliance went on to further its cause at a press conference held at the Radisson Fort George Hotel when the goals were presented:

- To claim a territorial sea to the median line in the south.
- To demand a referendum on the Maritime Areas Bill.
- To defend the territorial integrity of Belize and the constitutional rights of its citizens.
- To end the immigration of Central Americans.
- To end the secret granting of Belizean citizenship to foreigners without restriction.

The press conference was followed one week later, on December 17, 1991, with a rally in front of the Supreme Court building to mobilize opposition to the Maritime Areas Bill that was before the National Assembly. The first rumbling of political agitation was heard in Philip Goldson's address when he reminded those assembled that the name of the old Battlefield "has been renewed here in this spot where so many spiritual battles and so many political battles have been fought". He recalled "that old cry which used to ring out here more than 25 years ago: 'This is our country, we own it, we love it, and we will keep it. '"

National Alliance for Belizean Rights

The Patriotic Alliance for Territorial Integrity became a political party at a rally held on January 30, 1992 at the Cinderella Plaza. It was then officially named the National Alliance for Belizean Rights (N.A.B.R.). Goldson, who had resigned as Deputy Secretary General of the U.D.P. and who had served as National Coordinator of the Patriotic Alliance, was the nominal[56] Party Leader. He emphasized that N.A.B.R. would be concentrating on matters having to do with immigration, economic policies and Belize's relations with Guatemala.

Philip Goldson as Party Leader

N.A.B.R., in constituting itself as a political party, declared its foundation date to be January 13, 1992. Adopting the party colors of green and white its mission was declared to identify, defend, expand and activate Belizean rights; while its main

---

[56]Goldson preferred to be termed National Coordinator.

objective was to preserve the independence of Belize with its sovereignty established within the land and sea boundaries to which it is entitled under national and international law.

Within two months of its inception the Party was represented in every district. When Belizeans living abroad joined the struggle to keep Belize for Belizeans this resulted in N.A.B.R. having eight District Alliances within Belize along with a number of other districts organized by Belizeans abroad.

Amidst rumors that Philip Goldson would be rejoining the U.D.P. he denied these, emphatically stating that Belizeans needed the N.A.B.R. to support Belizean rights for the benefit of its people everywhere. It therefore became nationally accepted that there had occurred an irretrievable breakdown of relations between the U.D.P. and the breakaway leaders of N.A.B.R. This prompted speculations and questions on many fronts as to whether Belize needed a third political party; what a third party had to offer, or even could a third party win elections. Goldson's response was embodied in a demand he made in the House of Representatives on July 24, 1992 that N.A.B.R. be recognized as a third party. In support he referred to the fact that a delegation comprising representatives from the P.U.P. and the U.D.P. would be attending a Mexican/Belizean parliamentary conference in Mexico City in a few days and N.A.B.R. had not been included. It was a signal victory for the Party therefore when, on July 27, 1992, it received an invitation to attend the conference. Goldson and Aikman joined the delegation in Mexico City.

Recognition as a Third Party

While N. A. B. R's position as a third party was officially recognized when the Ministry of Foreign Affairs ruled that the Party would be represented at future Belize/Guatemala negotiations, from 1992 it also became a part of Belize's official September celebrations with Goldson addressing the gatherings as a part of the program.

In keeping with its motto "Only the Alliance of God and the People Can Save the People" N.A.B.R. established its own newspaper The Alliance Weekly. On the competitive front the Party selected Adelma Broaster to contest a by-election held on January 27, 1993 in the Freetown Division. She received 102 votes losing to both the P.U.P. and the U.D.P. candidates.

City Council Election 1993

In the City Council election on March 18, 1993, which was won by the P.U.P., the 9 N.A.B.R. candidates garnered just over 5% of the votes cast.

U. D. P-N.A.B.R. Coalition

Following an announcement by the British High Commissioner on May 13, 1993 that in about one year's time Britain would be withdrawing its troops from Belize, the U.D.P. and the N.A.B.R. met to propose the formation of a joint committee of the two parties to deal with the country's future security. The two parties took that opportunity to establish other areas of cooperation especially pledging not to oppose each other in the upcoming General Election. This move resulted in a U.D.P. -N.A.B.R. coalition winning 16 of the 29 seats in the House of Representatives when elections were held on June 30, 1993. Goldson retained his seat in the Albert Division and was appointed to the Cabinet as Minister of Human Resources. With a voice in the government N.A.B.R. soon after proposed that the clause in the Maritime Areas Act, which restricted the southern waters to three miles, be amended to give Belize its full territorial waters.

Other Election Results

In 1996 N.A.B.R. contested the Belize City Council election but was unsuccessful. The Party also contested the 1998 General Election and received only 174 of the total votes cast. Following the death of Philip Goldson on October 3, 2001 the N.A.B.R. remained relatively quiet in subsequent years and did not contest general elections in 2003, 2008 and 2012.

Ever since the official recognition of the N.A.B.R. in 1992 as a third political party in Belize several individuals took the bold initiative to establish parties to counter the perceived ills of the two established mass parties: the P.U.P. and the U.D.P. Their attempts to contest and win elections, even by forming alliances among themselves, proved unsuccessful.

The People's Democratic Party – 1995

The People's Democratic Party (P.D.P.) was formed in 1995 under the leadership of Estevan Perera and Deputy Leader Jose Sosa. Its primary aims were to introduce a different approach to Belize's party politics and develop a system of trust and cooperation between government and people.

With the appearing of the P.D.P. on the scene it was the first time in Belize's political history that four parties contested a Belize City Council election. The election was held on March 18, 1996 and, along with N.A.B.R., the P.D.P. influenced about 10% of the voters which had no material impact on the election results. It might have succeeded, however, in demonstrating some spark and sincerity by introducing refreshing new political talent.

The P.D.P. contested the 1998 General Election and received only 225 of the total votes cast. The Party did not contest the 2003, 2008 or the 2012 elections.

The National Reality Truth Creation Party – 1998

Described as a Christian party The National Reality Truth Creation Party was founded in 1998 by Jorge Ernesto Babb. Contesting the 1998 General Election the Party received seven votes. The Party did not contest the 2003 election, but did so in 2008 with no success.

Leading up to the 2008 General Election Babb returned to the political scene by contesting in the Freetown Division while endorsing Ebony Babb for the Queen's Square Division. On election- day, February 7, 2008, the Party received 29 votes.

We the People Reform Movement – 2003

Entering the political arena specifically to contest the General Election of March 5, 2003 was the We the People Reform Movement (W.T.P.). Styled as a movement of independent candidates[xxii] the W.T.P. had as its National Coordinator

Francis Gegg, with deputies Hipolito Bautista and Lucilo Teck. The main thrust of its campaign was constitutional, political, economic and social reform with emphasis on an elected Senate and equal electoral divisions. Worthy of note was that other prominent Belizeans had called for an elected Senate and that proposal had been included in a political reform report as early as 1999.

The W.T.P. fielded a total of 11 candidates for the 2003 General Election: two in Belize City, four in Corozal, one in Cayo, one in Orange Walk, two in Stann Creek and one in Toledo. On election-day, March 5, no seats were won.

In municipal elections held on March 1, 2006 the W.T.P. entered seven candidates, including one Mayoral candidate, in Corozal Town. Although the W.T.P. did not win any seats observers felt that its effect was to make the election race rather close for the first place U.D.P. In October 2007 the W.T.P., along with the People's National Party and the Party of Christians Pursuing Reform, formed a National Belizean Alliance to contest the 2008 General Election

Vision Inspired By the People – 2005

The Vision Inspired by the People (V.I.P.) officially came on the political scene when, on December 4, 2005, it introduced itself to residents of the City of Belmopan. The nominal Party Leader was Paul Morgan with Hubert Enriquez as Secretary General. Armed with a plan for the implementation of projects in Belmopan the V.I.P. presented a slate of candidates to contest the municipal elections scheduled for March 1, 2006.

Advocating a needed change for Belize the V.I.P. stated that a victory in Belmopan would be the seed to eventually remove corruption in the nation's capital. Predictably neither the P.U.P. nor the U.D.P. welcomed their new opponent; both accusing the other of instigating and supporting the V.I.P. to contest the election as a distraction for Belmopan residents.

The V.I.P. candidates, consisting of Paul Morgan, Bobby Lopez, Kamil Espat, Henry Dueck, David Gonzalez, Elvira Brown and Hubert Enriquez, did not win any seats in the municipal elections. The U.D.P. won all seven seats in Belmopan on its way to an overall countrywide victory of 64 to three. Analysts attributed the Party's lack of success to a low budget, inexperience in campaign and image management, and the apathy of Belmopan voters. The Party's candidates to contest the 2008 General Election were

Harrisford Myers	Belize Rural Central
Paul Morgan	Belmopan
Gilroy Requena	Cayo Central
Hubert Enriquez	Cayo South
Martha Hendricks	Cayo West
Patrick Rogers	Collet
Quentin Mejia	Dangriga
Joseph Martinez	Lake Independence
Erwin X Jones	Port Loyola
Mateo Polanco	Stann Creek West
Max Cho	Toledo West

Election-day was on February 7 and the V.I.P. received 874 votes, or 0.75% of the total votes cast.

The V.I.P. joined an alliance in 2011 with the People's National Party to form the Belize Unity Alliance (B.U.A.) to contest the general election scheduled for 2012. One candidate was announced for Belize Rural North in the person of Rufus X.

The People's National Party – 2007

A young political movement calling itself The People's National Party (P. N.P.) held its first meeting on February 19, 2007 in San Antonio Village, Toledo District. Declaring as candidates for the 2008 General Election were Party Leader Wil Meheia for Toledo East and Dionisio Choc for Toledo West. Running on a platform of anti-corruption and pro-environment the P. N.P., in March 2007, declared its intention to form a coalition with the V.I.P.

In October 2007 the P. N.P., along with the W.T.P. and the Party of Christians Pursuing Reform, formed a National Belizean Alliance to contest the 2008 General Election.

In 2011, the P. N.P., after joining with the V.I.P. to form the Belize Unity Alliance (B.U.A.) declared candidates in Toledo East (Wil Maheia), Stann Creek West (Basilio Mes) and Belize Rural South (Mike Campbell) to contest the general election scheduled for 2012.

The National Reform Party – 2007

Promoting itself as a Christian conservative political party seeking office in order to eradicate poverty, crime and corruption in Belize politics, The National Reform Party (N.R.P.) held a press conference on February 21, 2007 at its headquarters on the Northern Highway. Party Leader Cornelius Dueck presented the Party's platform as anti-corruption, pro-development and social uplifting while promising transparency about campaign financing.

The N.R.P. boldly displayed its Party colors of orange and white with the emblem of a fist enclosed by a circle depicting a combination of power, security, value, justice, unity, inclusiveness and togetherness.

Party Leader Dueck held the opinion that neither the ruling P.U.P. nor the Opposition U.D.P. had anything to offer Belizeans and with the following candidates his Party could make a change in the 2008 General Election:

Ernesto Caliz	Belize Rural South
George Boiton Jr.	Cayo Central
Alden McDougal	Cayo North
Cornelius Dueck	Cayo Northeast
Denton Castillo	Dangriga
Gary Lambey	Lake Independence
Alvaro Espejo	Orange Walk Central
Pabel Torres	Orange Walk East
Hilberto Nah	Orange Walk North
Edwardo Melendez	Orange Walk South
Fermin Choc	Toledo West

On election-day, February 7, 2008, the Party received 887 votes, or 0.76% of the votes cast.

National Belize Alliance – 2007

One of the more formal alliances entered into by political parties seeking to form a viable third party was the National Belize Alliance (N.B.A.). On October 1, 2007 three political leaders met at the Chateau Caribbean in Belize City and established the N.B.A. Representing their individual parties were Wil Meheia of the P. N.P. who was elected Leader, Hipolito Bautista of the W.T.P. as General Secretary, and Richard Smith of the Party of Christians Pursuing Reform[57] as Spiritual Leader. Dionisio Choc was elected as Ambassador for Indigenous Affairs.

Wil Meheia, in planning to build the N.B.A. into a fully representative, democratic, strong and viable force, saw the alliance as a development which the Belizean people had long been waiting for. He promised that the N.B.A. would work assiduously to introduce an elected multi-party House of Representatives and Senate to deliver the reforms, good governance and equal rights needed for so long.

In the 2008 General Election on February 7 the N.B.A. candidates were:

Richard Smith	Cayo South
Salustiano Lizama	Orange Walk South
Wil Maheia	Toledo East
Dionisio Chuc	Toledo West

On election-day, February 7, 2008, the N.B.A. garnered 506 votes, or 0.43% of the votes cast.

---

[57]A short-lived party which originated in San Ignacio

The Party of Christians Pursuing Reform – 2007

The Party of Christians Pursuing Reform was formed in October 2007 by a group from Cayo under Richard Smith. A group of third parties consisting of the People's National Party, We the People Reform Movement, and the Party of Christians Pursuing Reform formed a coalition called the National Belize Alliance to contest the 2008 general election.

Belize Unity Alliance – 2011

An alliance, entitled the Belize Unity Alliance (B.U.A.) was formed in November 2011 only to contest the next general election in March 2012. The B.U.A. comprised of the V.I.P. and the P. N.P. and other interested candidates did not represent a formal merge of the parties. Primarily aimed at contesting the general election, there existed a looser coalition for the 2012 municipal elections due in March 2012. Slates were earmarked for the P. N.P. in Dangriga and Punta Gorda, the V. I. P in Belmopan and Belize City, and independents in San Ignacio/Santa Elena and San Pedro.

Belize Progressive Party – 2015

In October 2015 a merger of several opposition parties created the Belize Progressive Party (B.P.P.), which made its electoral debut in the November 4, 2015 general election. The party got 2,336 votes or 1.65% of the total votes cast. Holding its inaugural National Party Congress on December 4, 2016, the B.P.P. elected an executive to replace its pro-tem body: Chairman – Paco Smith; Secretary General – Hipolito Bautista; Political Leaders – Patrick Faber and Wil Meheia.

SECTION SIX
2015 – A YEAR FOR ELECTIONS

An unprecedented spate of various elections took place during 2015, strengthening the U. D. P in most instances and causing pundits to voice grave concerns about the future of the P.U.P., as well as aspiring third parties.

Cayo By-Election

The Cayo North constituency held a by-election on January 5, 2015 to elect a successor to the P.U.P. Area Representative Joseph Mahmud, who had resigned in November 2014. The P.U.P. nominee, Richard Harrison, was defeated by the U.D.P. nominee, Omar Figueroa.

Dangriga By-Election

Following the resignation of the P.U.P. Area Representative Ivan Ramos on June 8, 2015, a by-election was held on July 8. The U.D.P. nominee Frank Mena garnered 57.89% of the votes, defeating the P.U.P. candidate Anthony Sabal and the Belize Green Independent Party's Llewellyn Lucas.

Municipal Election

Countrywide municipal elections were held on March 4, 2015. With only 60,533 out of 105,634 registered voters, the results revealed the U.D.P. winning majorities in Punta Gorda, Dangriga, Belize City, San Ignacio, Belmopan, Corozal, Benque

Viejo del Carmen, and San Pedro. The P.U.P. won the municipality of Orange Walk.

General Election

Prime Minister Barrow announced an early election to be held on November 4, 2015. On election-day the U. D. P won 19 seats to the P. U. P's 12. This caused the U.D.P. to win a third consecutive election for the first time in its history, and in the history of elections in Belize. Of interest is that although the P. N.P. merged with the V.I.P. and other opposition groups to form the Belize Progressive Party (B.P.P.), none of its 25 candidates were successful. Another party, the Belize Green Independent Party, fielded one candidate in Toledo East.

Figure 20 - Dean Barrow

CONCLUSION

The pattern of the majority of political parties opposed to the P.U.P. since 1951 was a history of amalgamations, coalitions and alliances. Apart from the two mass parties – the People's United Party and the United Democratic Party –the other parties formed between 1951 and 1969 in an opposition capacity and the smaller parties that existed between 1974 and 1988, along with Third Party hopefuls since 1991, no other political party has succeeded in forming the government of Belize.

Following the trend in Caribbean politics several countries, including Belize, have traditionally ousted long-ruling parties from government, and turned to a new generation of leaders. Political developments even point to countries talking about forming a Caribbean Union, based on the European Union pattern. Even though changes have taken place as far as third parties go, and there is a definite wind of change hanging in the air for Belize, it has to be realized that the two- party pattern of politics has reigned in Belize for many decades, and there is no indication that this will soon change. Even given three terms constitutionally the two mass parties will very likely continue to find themselves running the government alternately.

APPENDICES

Appendix I
The Institution of Adult Suffrage

Adult suffrage universally means "the right to vote".

Voting rights in Belize's history go back to the 18th century when regulations governing the Settlement had to be approved by a majority vote of the inhabitants at a Public Meeting. (At first only rich white men, then rich colored men were entitled to be members of the Public Meeting).

The present day Belize Legislature is a direct descendant of the Public Meeting. Historically, a Legislative Assembly met for the first time in January 1854 and of its 21 members 18 were elected and three officially nominated by the Superintendent (who later became termed as governor). From that time, to be a voter, persons (only men could vote until the 1935 Constitution gave women the right with limited franchises) had to own property valued at seven Pounds a year, or earn 100 Pounds a year. The situation of the Legislature being an entirely nominative body existed from 1871 when Belize became a Crown Colony, until the elective principle was returned through the Constitution of 1935.

Between 1935 and 1954 (when adult suffrage was instituted) voters had to be 21 years old; receive an income of $300.00 a year; or own property valued at $500.00; or be a householder paying rent of $97.00 a year. For this reason in 1936, for example, registered voters totaled 1,035 in a population of

56,000; and in 1945 there were only 822 registered voters in a population of 63,000.

So it was that in 1954, under a new constitution, it can be said that the struggle for democracy and self-government went in the people's favor. Even though the governor still had reserve powers, and elected members were a minority in the Executive Council, the Legislative Assembly now consisted of nine ELECTED members and six nominated.

The introduction of ADULT SUFFRAGE was the biggest triumph, and this revolutionized the political life of Belize. For too long the people had participated in politics without candidates (candidates were required to have property valued at $500.00 or an annual income of $1,000.00), without the benefit of a party, and to a great extent without a vote.

The 1954 Constitution succeeded in finally authorizing the mass participation of Belizeans in their own political affairs, gradually lifting the mantle of Crown Colony government and colonialism.

In 1960 the Ministerial system was introduced, with the elected representatives being a majority on the Executive Council.

With the attainment of Self-Government by the 1964 Constitution, the Legislative Assembly was renamed the House of Representatives.

Appendix II
The Webster Proposals

Article 1 of the draft treaty provided that British Honduras would be granted independence under the name of Belize not later than 31st December 1970.

Article 2 obliged Belize and Guatemala to grant to each other's goods free entry through their ports and free transit through predetermined routes of each country.

Under Article 3, the port of Belize City would be declared a duty free port for the benefit of Guatemala and placed under the control of a supra-national Authority. Guatemala was obliged, at the request of Belize, to provide similar facilities for Belizean goods.

Article 4 guaranteed nationals of each country free movement in the territory of the other as well as the right to the same treatment as was accorded by each country to its own citizens. This included the right to freely acquire and dispose of personal real property.

Under Article 9, Guatemala and Belize agreed to establish a supra-national Authority to be charged with the responsibility of carrying out certain powers and functions including the supervision and control of free ports, as well as the designation of transit routes. Britain was required to pay to the Authority US$4m. to assist the Authority to perform its functions under the Treaty.

Article 10 provided that Belize would join CACM before 31st December 1970 with financial assistance from Britain.

Article 13 obliged Guatemala and Belize to consult and cooperate with each other on such matters of national concern in foreign affairs as may be raised by either government.

According to Article 14, the defense of Belize would be handled within the framework of the Inter-American Treaty of 1947, to which Belize would accede. In that event it would not be necessary for Belize to conclude bilateral defense arrangements with any other country.

The proposals were totally unacceptable to Belize primarily on the grounds that:

Defense, foreign affairs and, to a lesser extent the economy of Belize would be placed under Guatemalan control after independence.

Belize would be exclusively committed to a hemispheric destiny as a satellite or department of Guatemala.

Very few concessions were made to the dominant traditional social values.

Because of the great disparity between Guatemala and Belize in terms of population and resources the treaty would result in the effective domination of Belize by Guatemala.

Appendix III
Results of General Elections 1984 – 2015

Results of General Election 14 December 1984

Parties	Votes	%	Seats
United Democratic Party	25,756	54.07	21
People's United Party	20,961	44.00	7
Christian Democratic Party	708	1.49	-
Independents	213	0.44	-
Total valid votes	47,638	100.00	28
Invalid votes	673		
Total votes cast	**48,311**		

Registered voters – 64,447   *Turnout – 74.9%*

Results of General Election 4 September 1989

Parties	Votes	%	Seats
People's United Party	29,986	50.87	15
United Democratic Party	28,900	49.02	13
Independents	65	0.11	-
Total valid votes	58,951	100.00	28
Invalid votes	1,003		
Total votes cast	**59,954**		

Registered voters – 82,556   *Turnout – 72.6%*

Results of General Election 30 June 1993

Parties	Votes	%	Seats
United Democratic Party/National Alliance for Belizean Rights	34,306	48.70	16
People's United Party	36,082	51.20	13
Independents	43	0.10	-
Total valid votes	70,431	100.00	29
Invalid votes	499		
Total votes cast	**70,930**		

Registered voters – 98,371   *Turnout – 72.1%*

225

Results of General Election 27 August 1998

Parties	Votes	%	Seats
People's United Party	50,330	59.67	26
United Democratic Party	33,237	39.41	3
People's Democratic Party	225	0.27	-
National Alliance for Belizean Rights	174	0.21	-
National Reality Truth Creation Party	7	0.00	-
Independents	372	0.44	-
Total valid votes	84,345	100.00	29
Invalid votes	544		
Total votes cast	**84,889**		

Registered voters – 94,143   Turnout – 90.1%

Results of General Election 5 March 2003

Parties	Votes	%	Seats
People's United Party	52,934	53.16	22
United Democratic Party	45,376	45.57	7
Independents	1,260	1.27	-
Total valid votes	99,570	100.00	29
Invalid votes	770		
Total votes cast	**100,340**		

Registered voters – 126,202   Turnout – 79.5%

Results of General Election 7 February 2008

Parties	Votes	%	Seats
United Democratic Party	66,203	56.61	25
People's United Party	47,624	40.72	6
National Reform Party	887	0.76	-
Vision Inspired by the People	874	0.75	-
National Belize Alliance (including People's National Party)	506	0.43	-
Independents	71	0.06	-
National Reality Truth Creation Party	29	0.02	-
Total valid votes	116,194		31
Invalid votes	749		
Total votes cast	116,943		

Registered voters – 157,993   Turnout – 74.49%

Results of General Election 7 March 2012

Parties	Votes	%	Seats
United Democratic Party	64,976	50.43	17
People's United Party	61,832	47.99	14
People's National Party	828	0.64	-
Independents	822	0.64	-
Vision Inspired by the People	382	0.30	-
Total valid votes	128,840	100.00	31
Invalid votes	1,463		
Total votes cast	**130,303**		

Registered voters – 178,054   Turnout – 73.18%

Results of General Election 4 November 2015

Parties	Votes	%	Seats
United Democratic Party	71,452	50.52	19
People's United Party	67,566	47.77	12
Belize Progressive Party	2,336	1.65	0
Belize Green Independent Party	5	0.01	0
Independents	72	0.05	0
Total valid votes	41,431	100.00	31
Invalid votes	1,450		
Total votes cast	142,881		

Registered voters – 196,587   Turnout – 72.68%

INDEX OF POLITICAL PARTIES

Belize Popular Party 204
Belize Progressive Party 217
Belize Unity Alliance.. 217
Christian Democratic Party 175, 203
Corozal United Front... 203
Corozal United Party 203
Democratic Agricultural and Labour Party................................ 175
Honduran Independence Party... 138
National Alliance for Belizean Rights 205
National Belize Alliance... 216
National Independence Party 143
National Party 129
National Reality Truth Creation Party 211
National Reform Party 214
Party of Christians Pursuing Reform 217
People's Democratic Party... 210
People's Development Movement 187
People's National Party... 214
People's United Party... 32
Peoples' Independent Party.. 180
San Pedro United Movement 204
Toledo Progressive Party 203
United Black Association for Development 180
United Democratic Party... 190
Vision Inspired By the People 212
We the People Reform Movement... 211

REFERENCES

Alliance Weekly 1992 –

Amandala 1970 –

The Beacon 1970 –

The Belize Billboard 1950 – 1970

The Belize Times 1956 –

The Daily Clarion 1949 – 1961

The Reporter 1968 –

FURTHER READING

Barry, Tom and Vernon, Dylan, 1995. 2 ed. Inside Belize. Albuquerque: Resource Center Press.

Grant, Cedric H., 1976. The making of modern Belize: Politics, society and British Colonialism in Central America. Cambridge University Press.

MacPherson, Anne S., 2009. From colony to nation: women activists and the gendering of politics in Belize, 1912-1982. Lincoln: University of Nebraska Press.

Merrill, Tim, ed., 1992. Belize: a country study. Washington: GPO for the Library of Congress.

Palacio, Myrtle, 2011. Politics in Belize: the naked truth. Belize City: Glessima Research Services.

Peedle, Ian, 1999. Belize: A guide to the people, politics and culture. Northampton: Interlink Books.

Pollard, Nicholas Jr., 2011. Understanding the role of the Christian trade unions in the making of modern Belize: A historical perspective. Belmopan: Print Belize.

Shoman, Assad, 1987. Party politics in Belize. Benque Viejo: Cubola Productions.

Shoman, Assad, 1994. Thirteen chapters of a history of Belize. Belize City: Angelus Press.

Waddell, D. A. G., 1961. British Honduras: a historical and contemporary survey. Westport: Greenwood Press.

END NOTES

---

[i] Antonio Soberanis has gone down in Belize's history as the one who started the cry for independence. He was born in San Antonio, Orange Walk District, Belize, of Mexican parents in 1897 and died in 1975. In 1934 he defied the colonial powers by launching a series of strikes in an effort to improve working conditions. These strikes were important milestones for Belize in that they gave birth to a nationalistic movement which led up to the struggle for independence. Soberanis was responsible for organizing a movement called the *Labor and Unemployed Association (LUA)* with about 5000 members. The movement, which Soberanis himself described as a political party, was short-lived (1934-1936) because the colonial powers found ways to silence him by imprisonment and charges of seditious intention; but nevertheless it was sufficient to allow him to confront the social and economic issues of that time and got the people to thinking seriously.

[ii] A porridge consisting of boiled rice with sugar.

[iii] This remark was not an idle one, because actually the then Chief Justice, C. W. Greenidge, and Alan Burns disliked each other intensely, and Greenidge had always gone out of his way to upset the administration by interpreting the law very liberally and letting miscreants go free that the administration wanted locked up.

[iv] Today the site of Battlefield Park in Belize City, during the early days of the Belize Settlement the 'Battlefield' served as a popular site for the labor movement, political meetings and public assemblies.

[v] St. George's Caye, which is located about 20 minutes by boat from Belize City, was the scene of a battle between the British settlers (Baymen) and the Spaniards on September 10, 1798 for control of Belize. The island was first populated by buccaneers, and the British made it the capital of the Belize Settlement between 1650 and 1784. The Battle of St. George's Caye was the last time that Spain attempted to gain control over Belize; however, although the legal status of the settlement did not change it did not become a colony of Britain until 1862. Officially declared as a national holiday since 1898, September 10 is commemorated every year with much fanfare.

[vi] The Legislative Council was a body that dated back to the 19th century history of Belize. Previously administered by a rudimentary form of government called the Public Meeting, a new constitution in 1854

replaced it with a Legislative Assembly with 18 elected members. By the end of the decade the Legislative Assembly requested crown colony status hoping that the British would take on more of the defense costs. To accommodate such status, the Legislative Assembly voted in 1870 to replace itself with an appointed Legislative Council. The constitution of 1954, which introduced adult suffrage, also replaced the Legislative Council with a Legislative Assembly that had 9 elected, 3 official and 3 appointed members, while establishing an Executive Council chaired by the Governor.

[vii] The Commission of Inquiry appointed in 1948 to make recommendations on constitutional advance did not submit its report until April 1951. Drafting of constitutional instruments did not proceed until after January 1953, and the new constitution came into effect in 1954. The three-year period of the Legislative Council was therefore prolonged by the Governor, until elections could be held under the new constitution.

[viii] When the Executive Council was established under the 1954 constitution its nine members were taken from the Legislative Assembly and included the three official members, two of the appointed members, and four of the elected members chosen by the Legislative Assembly. The Governor was required to abide by the advice of the Executive Council, but he still held reserve powers and controlled the introduction of financial measures into the legislature.

[ix] "A Report of an Inquiry held by Sir Reginald Sharpe Q. C. into allegations of contacts between the People's United Party and Guatemala" is a Parliamentary Report that investigated the activities of George Price and other leaders of the P.U.P. with respect to their relations with the leftist government of Jacobo Arbenz in Guatemala.

[x] In a published statement released following the split it was revealed that the leaders of the P.U.P. did not leave the Party because they so much objected to Party policy, but because of Nicholas Pollard's alleged dishonesty in the General Workers Union.

[xi] Francisco Sagastume was a political opponent of Guatemalan President Ramon Ydigoras Fuentes. He had in 1958 staged an unsuccessful 'liberation mission' to Benque Viejo in western Belize. Arriving in Pueblo Viejo in January 1962 Sagastume, hoping to spark an uprising against the British, announced that liberation was at hand and proceeded to burn photographs of Queen Elizabeth, the Duke of Edinburgh, and the Union Jack. Encountering hostility from the villagers, whose ancestors had fled

from Guatemala three generations before, he advanced more into Belize territory to the town of Punta Gorda where he and his followers were arrested. Sentenced to 10 years of hard labor, he returned to Guatemala after serving only one year in prison. Sagastume went on to become elected to the Guatemalan Congress.

[xii] Price's frequent allusions to the United Nations were most likely based on the historic 1960 United Nations resolution which fully supported independence for colonial territories. Significantly, the Caribbean countries of Jamaica and Trinidad and Tobago became independent in 1962; and it was time for Belize to become independent also.

[xiii] Gwendolyn Lizarraga was the first woman elected to serve in the House of Representatives. She served for three terms, being first elected in 1961 and serving as Minister of Education from 1965-1969. She died on June 9, 1975, at the age of 74.

[xiv] The main factor was that the government of Guatemala insisted on a land claim to Belize, and threatened to use force against Belize if it became independent without first settling the claim.

[xv] Between 1975 and 1979 the U. S. A. abstained on all the United Nations resolutions concerning Belize's independence and territorial integrity. In 1980 it finally shifted its position and voted in favor of the United Nations resolution calling for the independence of Belize.

[xvi] The "Heads of Agreement" document stated that there was no final agreement to the Guatemalan claim, but there was room for further discussions to form the basis for a final agreement. Within the 16 clauses of the 'agreement' Guatemala agreed to recognize an independent Belize within its existing borders, but only if agreement could be reached on other points in the document. Other points included: the use and enjoyment of certain cayes, free port facilities, free transit on two roads, facilitation of oil pipelines, cooperation in security, and a non-aggression pact.

[xvii] At a subsequent meeting the N.I.P. Executive Committee decided not to accept the proposal, the reason being that the P.U.P. - C.D.U. members in Government were supposed to be the ones responsible for solving the unemployment problem and it would be farcical to associate with the Union in a protest against their own members in Government.

[xviii] The N.I.P. had asked the Governor and the Secretary of State to allow the Party to be represented by more than one delegate allocated to it by Government. The P.U.P. would be represented by four delegates and an adviser while the N.I.P. had been relegated to one delegate and an

adviser. In reply the Secretary of State said he could not allow the Party more than one delegate and, since constitutional conferences were not determined by votes of delegates, the representation agreed for the N.I.P. was sufficient to enable it to make its case. Furthermore representation at constitutional conferences was usually confined to parties with elected members in an Assembly. In view of the electoral support the N.I.P. got in the general election in 1961 the Secretary of State felt that the allocation of one representative was reasonable.

[xix] The D.A.L.P. was more commonly referred to as the Christian Democratic Party because it was said to promote Christian Democratic ideals. Interestingly enough, in the 1984 general election, the name 'C.D.P.' was briefly revived by Dangriga candidate Theodore Aranda to promote his new party based in Dangriga.

[xx] Evan X Hyde received 89 votes which observers viewed as the margin of victory that swung to the P.U.P. by one vote and cost the U.D.P. one of the three seats that might have caused a deadlock in the House of Representatives.

[xxi] The Corozal United Front was formed in 1974 under Israel Alpuche. It was active only in Corozal and became an affiliate of the United Democratic Party.

[xxii] Election 2003 was dubbed 'the year of the Independents' because it was the first time as many as 25 candidates were running as independents. Apart from the 17 candidates for the General Election, there were five for the Belmopan Town Council and three for the Belize City Council. None were successful.

ABOUT THE AUTHOR

Lawrence Vernon is a career librarian whose ambition since his appointment to the National Library Service in 1956 has been to strengthen and expand the public libraries network in Belize, and improve access to relevant information and education by all Belizeans especially children and special needs groups. His ongoing contribution is the restructuring and equipping of the Belize National Library Service, as well as the eleven years he spent at the University of Belize Library, to allow for greater institutional competencies, and to develop their organizational capacities for financial sustainability.

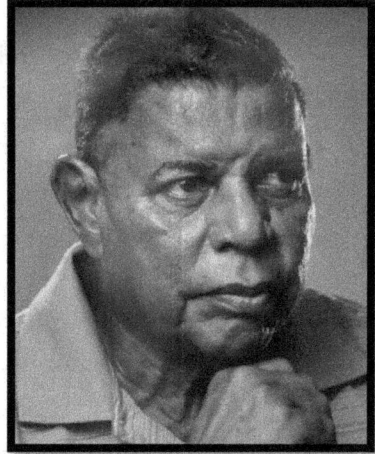

In community services he has chaired the National Honors and Awards Advisory Committee, and been involved in key positions with:
- The Council of Voluntary Social Services
- Excelsior High School
- The Belize Book Industry Association
- The National Advisory Committee for the Virtual Health Library
- The Belize National Commission for UNESCO
- The Belize Archives and Records Service Advisory Board

Apart from writing and having some of his short stories published, his more recent endeavors have taken him into the realm of research writing and publication, some of which are:

- Cultural Groups of Belize
- Dreadlocks Displaced
- The Andy Palacio Moment
- A Walk through Old Belize
- Placencia and its Environs

He has edited and reviewed several works by national authors, which have been published in <u>Belizean Studies</u> and the <u>Amandala</u> newspaper. Lawrence feels that although Belize's literary output is relatively still small, the benefits that both young and older library users have derived, and are deriving, from reading will accrue to Belize's continued educational and informational development.